Unlocking the Mysteries of
Sensory Dysfunction

A resource for anyone who works with, or lives with, a child with sensory issues

by

Elizabeth Anderson

&

Pauline Emmons

Future Horizons, Inc.

Future Horizons, Inc.
721 W. Abram Street
Arlington, TX 76013

800-489-0727; 817-277-0727
817-277-2270 Fax

Website: www.FutureHorizons-autism.com
E-mail: edfuture@onramp.net

ISBN # 1-885477-25-2

Dedication

We dedicate this book to Ellie and Dylan: our two Super Heroes

Contents

Foreword

by Thomas A. McKean

Since the initial conception of Sensory Integration Disorder by A. Jean Ayres, both the fundamentals and the more technical aspects of this disorder have plagued parents, professionals, teachers and most of all, those afflicted themselves.

I have lived with this disorder all of my short thirty years. Through various accommodations such as sleeping with heavy blankets and bears, wearing pressure bracelets, and holding onto my friends for dear life, I have gradually been able to live certainly not a "normal," but a life where I can at least live independently and on my own.

I didn't even know I had autism until five years ago. My response, of course, was to join the national board of directors of the Autism Society of America. This is where I first heard of sensory integration. At first, I ignored it. I felt the whole concept was over my head and only for those who were far smarter than myself. But the more I heard about it the more I began to listen. And the more I listened, the more my life began to make sense. Not in the sense that it made sense, but more in the sense that it made sense that it didn't make sense, if that in itself could be said to make sense.

So after I understood what was happening, and why, I began looking for my own answers, much as the authors of this book did. I found toothpaste I could actually use without throwing up, I found the common bond between the foods I could tolerate eating (soft texture), and through Temple Grandin's research into proprioception (see page three), I found that pressure bracelets did a great job of keeping me in reality.

Though it may well be said that most of you already know, either by research or by instinct, what is in here, it has never been written more clearly, nor has it been more easily defined. I believe A. Jean Ayres would be very proud of this work.

This book will not give you the technical aspects of SI. It will not talk about confusing neuro-motor pathways or chemical imbalances or various neuro transmitters. What it will tell you is what you need to know. What SI is, how it can go wrong, and what you can do about it if it does go wrong. That is all you will find here.

For many, this will be a relief. This is because most of the books written about SI (and there have been many, including my own) have been accused of "overkill." There is no overkill in these pages. What you will find is what you need to know. No more, and certainly, no less.

As I write this, I am visiting a family in Massachusetts who has a child with Autism. I have learned through them (and visiting other families like them) insight into what it is like to be the parent of a child with a disability. The problems with school, the endless hours in the bathroom, and the staying awake all night when you have a job to be at early in the morning. This can make life extremely rough. But then I have also watched many little miracles happen around the country with these kids, and I think just about all parents will tell you those little miracles make it all worthwhile.

Most of these children are extremely bright. Many have IQ's that fall into the genius category. Yet by some cosmic spin of the joke dial, they just do not seem to understand the world around them. They know WHAT is going on around them, far more clearly than anyone else. What they do not know, and what they NEED to know, is WHY these things are happening around them. As different as each child with Sensory Integration Disorder is, one universal truth (perhaps the ONLY universal truth) is that built deeply inside them there is an incredibly strong need to know "why."

They are smart enough to ask the why questions that no one else dares ask. They ask themselves only. And only because they know that no one else would understand the question, "Why are there wars?"

"Why do people fight and die over land and food when there is enough to share?" "Why does the color of your skin make a difference in how you are treated?" "Why are there homeless people walking the streets?" "Why doesn't someone do something about it?" "Why does love feel so good and so bad at the same time?" "Why am I upset when people I love die?" "Am I upset because they will no longer experience life, or am I upset because I will miss them?" "Whatever did become of Barrabus after Jesus was crucified?"

Thousands and thousands of "why" and "what" and "when" and "where" questions. ("Where HAVE all the flowers gone?") The very smartest of the smart ask more questions than the others. Yet they never once look for answers. This is because they are smart enough to know answers will not be found. All of these questions, and many, many others. You put them all together and you have something called "humanity." People with Sensory Integration Disorder will never be able to understand humanity. Yet even though they will not look for answers to those tough questions, they will also never stop trying to figure humanity out. So though they will never understand, many of them will understand better than the majority of people on earth, and at a very young age. The sadness in all of this is that most of them will never realize it.

If you are searching for answers to your child's pain, you may find it within these pages. I know this pain as well as any of them do. I also know that in spite of (or maybe because of) that pain, all children (and adults) with Sensory Integration Disorder have been given three wonderful gifts by God that a lot of the general population does not have. They have inner strength, they have incredible courage, and they have the potential and ability to be at peace with themselves and who they are.

These qualities are obvious to anyone who knows them, yet they are elusive to the people themselves. They need to be pointed out and developed and built upon. They need to be discovered by those who have them. Once they have discovered these three qualities within themselves, they are on the way to a journey through life that is far richer and more enjoyable than most people could ever dream of.

Sensory Integration Disorder can be a problem. But it can also be an asset. Either way, it is certainly not the end of the world. We all need to be reminded of this from time to time.

Let this book be that reminder for you.

Thomas A. McKean
Former member, ASA board of directors
Author, "Soon Will Come The Light"
Future Education Inc., Arlington, Texas

Diagnosed with Autism at age 14, Thomas was placed in a mental institution for a period of three years. Following this, Thomas has written a nationally award-winning book "Soon Will Come the Light." He has served on the national board of Autism Society of America and continues to advocate for Autism and Sensory Integration by speaking and writing.

Preface

This book was written for children; our children, and all children. We hope this book provides valuable insight into the world of a child with sensory issues. Our focus here is to understand this child's unique perspective, and its ramifications both at home and at school. Good luck as you embark upon your journey.

Sincerely,

Liz and Polly

Acknowledgements

With our deepest appreciation to: our husbands--Richard and Dale
our children--Lindy, Ellie, Julia, Carter, Dylan and Laura
our parents--Sissy and George, Frances and John
and to Eileen, Ellie and Dylan's occupational therapist.

A special thank you to Kathy, Tiffany, and the guardian angels who watch over us all.

Introduction

As mothers of children with Sensory Integration Disorder, we needed to write this book, not only to educate others, but to let our stories be known. We felt driven to share our experiences of living with a child with this disorder because we have both known its loneliness and frustration. We were unable to find information on Sensory Integration Disorder that was not highly technical, and were offered almost no guidance as we entered into the world of evaluations, Special Education committee meetings and therapy.

When our paths first crossed, each of us realized we shared a common bond, that of having a child diagnosed with Sensory Integration Disorder. The question then arose, "Are there common experiences for both the children and parents who live with Sensory Integration Disorder?" The answer was a resounding "YES!" Our goal in writing this book is to help other parents cope with the symptoms of this disorder, share this common bond, and rescue someone else from the dark abyss that we were trapped in for years.

This book is, in essence, a reflection of the young lives of our children, Ellie and Dylan. We think of these children as Super Heroes, because we cannot imagine what strength and courage it takes for them to cope with their disorder. We've often wondered what it must be like to be uncomfortable with hugs and kisses from a parent, or to experience a "fight or flight" sensation every time you are faced with the daily activities of brushing teeth or washing and combing hair.

Ellie and Dylan, like most children exhibiting the collection of symptoms of Sensory Integration Disorder, undergo occupational therapy several times a week just to help them function day-to-day. Each day they are confronted by their demons which come in the form of heightened sensitivities, coordination problems, developmental delays and a poor self-concept. As their mothers, we hope to help them fight their fears by drawing upon the strength and courage we know they already possess.

Sensory Integration

Because they understand their child usually better than anyone else, parents are often the first to sense when their child is struggling or suffering. While it may take months, or even years, to acknowledge or act on this "gut" feeling, many parents later confess that they sensed there was something different about this child at a very early age.

There is nothing easy about growing up. Some suffering and struggling are simply a part of childhood. For most children, these difficult periods are brief, merely a "stage" they are going through. But, for children with Sensory Integration Disorder, the struggle can seem never-ending and suffering a way of life.

There are a myriad of reasons why some children experience problems during the natural course of development: a genetic predisposition, a complication during pregnancy, or a difficult delivery, to name just three. In addition, current research is exploring other avenues: the possibility of a link between sensory integration and antibiotics, environmental toxins, allergies and childhood immunizations. While the causes of the collection of symptoms of Sensory Integration Disorder are still not clear to the medical and scientific communities, the resultant behaviors can be cataloged and diagnosed. One means of gauging whether or not Sensory Integration Disorder may be present is to observe how successfully a child is interacting with his or her environment.

All of the information children receive from their environment comes to them through the sensory systems. Although many people are familiar with the senses involved in taste, smell, sight and sound, most do not know that the nervous system also senses touch, movement, the force of gravity and body position. Each of these senses is critical to a child's ability to function in any environment: home, school, the playground, etc. For not only does processing information through the senses generate activity in the brain, but each of the senses acts as a stabilizing influence on the nervous system.

Since the brain directs all of the activity in both the mind and the body, when the brain is not integrating information from the senses well, a child's whole being is affected. When a child cannot process or respond appropriately to these incoming sensations, it is referred to as Sensory Integration Disorder or Sensory Integration Dysfunction.

The Sensory Systems

All children have sensory systems which use receptors to pick up information that is then processed by the brain. For example, structures within the inner ear detect movement and the nerves within the skin detect touch.

The sense of touch, called the **tactile** sense, makes it possible to determine if something is hot or cold, rough or smooth, sharp or dull. It is the tactile sense that also allows a child to feel something in the dark or to discriminate, without looking, between, the pleasurable sensation of tickling and the potentially dangerous one of a bee.

The **vestibular** sense coordinates the movement of the eyes, head and body. The brain then responds to this movement through space and body position. The vestibular sense allows a child to balance, kick a ball, or stumble without falling. In addition, this sensory system maintains muscle tone, coordinates the two sides of the body and enables a child to hold his head up against the forces of gravity.

The sense of **proprioception** uses unconscious information from the muscles and joints to give awareness of body position. This sense makes it possible for a child to guide her arm without watching the complete range of movement. It is proprioception that automatically adjusts body position to prevent a child from falling out of a chair and also allows a child to manipulate a pencil or comb.

Not only is it critical to a child's well-being that the sensory systems function properly, but that these systems work well together. If the tactile, vestibular and proprioceptive systems cannot function efficiently, either separately or together, it directly affects a child's ability to interact successfully with the surrounding environment.

If the tactile sensory system is not functioning efficiently, a child may have difficulty processing light or discriminatory touch stimuli. This difficulty can, for example, greatly hinder the development of the child's grapho-motor skills. As a result, this child may be unable to efficiently process the sensation of holding a pencil and, therefore, have difficulty writing. Or, an inefficient tactile sensory system may hinder a child in initiating and developing friendships. For example, a child may have such trouble discriminating touch stimuli that he responds violently to another child slightly bumping his arm. Responding in such a manner makes it extremely difficult for this child to be understood or liked by his peers. Similarly, if a child is uncomfortable sitting on the rug in her room, or the carpet in the classroom, it may be because she is unable to tolerate the texture due to her tactile defensiveness.

If the vestibular sensory system is not functioning efficiently, a child may have trouble planning an action. If a child has trouble planning an action, he will undoubtedly have difficulty performing this action. And, since a child draws upon past experience whenever a new task is to be performed, the problem only magnifies. For example, if a child has trouble planning how to get on a bicycle, this child will most likely have difficulty when it comes time to actually get on. If the child has a hard time planning how to get on and then riding a bike, this same child is almost certain to experience trouble when trying to ride a friend's bike. Similarly, if a child has difficulty going up or down the stairs at home, she will most likely have difficulty getting on and off the school bus, or climbing up and down the school's stairs.

If the proprioceptive sensory system is not functioning efficiently, a child may have difficulty engaging successfully in sports. If a child is unable to guide her arm to swing a bat without watching the arm, then this child will either watch the ball and not successfully swing the bat, or watch the range of arm motion to successfully swing the bat, but miss the pitch. Similarly, a child who is constantly fidgeting in his seat, or having to "contort" to stay in his seat, may also be responding to an inefficient proprioceptive system.

In order for a child with the symptoms of Sensory Integration Disorder to succeed academically, socially and athletically, it is imperative that the tactile, vestibular and proprioceptive sensory systems function well together.

Because of its complex nature, a poor self-image combined with emotional and behavioral problems is common in children with Sensory Integration Disorder. While this disorder affects an untold number of children, it is a

4

relatively new concept in the field of child development. Therefore, it is not well known to parents, educators, psychologists, or pediatricians.

Time Line

Infancy

The developmental time line is the foundation upon which most parents, teachers, psychologists and pediatricians base their expectations. This developmental time line is universal, it is applicable to children of all races, colors and creeds. This time line is not rigid, rather it is reflective of the fact that every child is different and will usually reach a given developmental milestone within a certain range of time. For example, the developmental time line states that a child will begin to walk between 10 and 14 months of age, with the average being 12 months of age. Thus, it is generally accepted that a child who starts walking at nine months is an early walker, while the child who starts walking at 15 months is a late walker.

Every "normal" adult began life as an infant, then reached adulthood by passing various developmental, emotional and intellectual milestones. Certain behaviors are expected during each stage of life. For example, a toddler is expected to throw tantrums and be a messy eater. In contrast, a school-age child is expected to have few tantrums and to eat proficiently using utensils.

Normal infant behaviors run the gamut. A baby may be very active, or very quiet. He may be easy or difficult to calm. She may seem a creature of routine or thrive on spontaneity. All of these behaviors are considered, and could be, normal. However, it could also be as early as infancy that parents start to get a "gut" feeling that something may be wrong with their child.

Most parents experience exhaustion and confusion whenever there is an infant in the house. If this is the first child, then the whole experience is new and confusing. If this child is not a first child, then the parents also have to cope with the demands of another child, in addition to meeting the demands of a new baby. It is because of this chaos, that some children with Sensory Integration Disorder may not stand out in an alarming fashion in infancy, or any other single developmental phase. Rather, they may only appear "odd" or "a little left of center."

However, other children with Sensory Integration Disorder do exhibit extremes of behavior even as early as infancy. Not wanting to be touched or cuddled is one common symptom. A baby who never sleeps, or who does not develop a pattern for eating and sleeping may also be exhibiting early signs of a sensory integration problem. An infant who takes an unusually long time to nurse or drink a bottle could be showing signs. Some infants with sensory integration problems become hysterical rocking in the baby swing or riding in the car.

Poor strength and coordination are two additional signs of Sensory Integration Disorder that can also be seen early on. A baby with Sensory Integration Disorder may have difficulty lifting its head when placed on its tummy or become frustrated trying to roll over, especially back to tummy. Symptoms of a potential fine motor delay can often be seen in the infant who has trouble manipulating toys or guiding a rattle successfully to her mouth.

Usually, the clues that an infant is experiencing sensory integration difficulties are there early on, if only parents knew how to recognize them. Imagine what it must be like to be aversive to touch, yet the more the infant cries, the more a parent tries to cuddle him. Or, to be an infant who has trouble sleeping for an extended period of time simply because she cannot tolerate the feeling of being swaddled. Or, the infant who fusses so much the parents take him for a car ride to calm him down, not realizing that the motion of the car only stimulates him even more.

Many parents acknowledge their child's infancy as a time of learning by trial and error. Because babies cannot verbalize what is bothering them, it is often anyone's guess. If the infant exhibiting symptoms of a sensory integration problem is the first child, the parents may wonder what they are doing wrong. If the infant is the second or third child, the parents may question what they are doing differently. However, with this disorder, it is not the parents who are different, it is the baby.

If you are a parent right now and are becoming uneasy reading this, relax. Listen to your "gut" feelings and keep on observing your infant. Only time will tell if there is truly cause for alarm. Discuss your feelings with your pediatrician so that you can begin making observations as a team. If you are wondering about the infant behavior of your now toddler or pre-school child, take a closer look, it could reveal a valuable diagnostic clue.

Toddlers

Life with a toddler is like riding a roller coaster. Life with a toddler who has Sensory Integration Disorder is like walking on a tightrope with someone vibrating both ends back and forth. Even if speech delays are present, the toddler and pre-school years are a time when most children begin to communicate effectively. Parents may not always like what their toddler has to say, but can understand it nonetheless. For a child with Sensory Integration Disorder, as the lines of communication increase, so can the child's cry for help. As a toddler's symptoms begin to manifest themselves differently or grow in number, it can be particularly frightening to parents.

Most everyone is familiar with the "terrible twos," a time when children begin exerting some control over their lives and the word "no" is used often. Children say "no" to tell their parents they do not like what they are being asked to do. Parents are usually able to distract or reason with their toddler to overcome this basic opposition to most everything. In contrast, when a child is in the "terrible twos" and also suffers from Sensory Integration Disorder, "no" may not mean "I don't want to," but, "I cannot tolerate this."

It is important to keep in mind that there is a wide range of what is considered "normal" behavior for a toddler. Many children at this age experience tantrums on a regular basis. Some children experience them several times a day, while others only once in a while. Some toddlers have outgoing personalities and others are shy, feeling more comfortable sticking close to Mom or Dad. One toddler may race down the walk while another jogs tentatively. Some children speak volumes at an early age, yet others take longer to develop fluent speech. Some toddlers may be content to spend hours in the sandbox or on the swings, for others, a few minutes is enough. Or, some toddlers may love to "draw," while others are simply not interested.

All of the above attributes are considered within normal range. It is when a toddler's behavior appears to be "abnormal," or simply does not follow the natural course of development that there may be reason for concern. Perhaps the toddler throws several severe temper tantrums a day, experiences drastic mood swings, trips often just walking or has speech that can only be understood by family members. A child who screams when placed in the sandbox or on a swing, or who refuses to even hold a crayon, are additional reasons for concern.

Remember, even some "typical" children can fit these descriptions. That is why it is so important to keep a running catalog of observations when parents suspect a problem. It is when the infant who displays abnormal behaviors grows into a toddler who displays more, or intensified, abnormal behaviors, that an evaluation is in order.

During the toddler years, many additional symptoms of Sensory Integration Disorder may appear. A child may have even more difficulty motor planning or crash into things. A child may also develop strong food preferences, have difficulty manipulating utensils or spill often. For some children with sensory integration problems, washing or combing their hair, cutting their fingernails or brushing their teeth are sensations they cannot tolerate. For other children, temperature preferences may become noticeable during the toddler years. As self-dressing develops, a child may also experience difficulty or make unusual clothing choices. For example, a child might require the outfit have nothing tight around the waist, wrists or neck, no tags and be a certain material. Subconsciously, by the time a child reaches pre-school age, most parents or childcare providers have learned to work around these bizarre behaviors without even having recognized their existence.

Pre-School

The pre-school years are often a time of delineation for a child (and parent) in many areas. By pre-school, a child has evolved into a disctinct little person, socially, emotionally, physically and developmentally. It is during these years that many children begin to venture out into the world and participate in organized activities outside of the home. This venturing out exposes a child not only to a variety of people and personal styles, but to the experience of being part of a group. It is in these group activities that pre-schoolers are often expected to "tow the line" and begin to meet new standards of behavior.

In this environment of higher expectations, a pre-schooler with Sensory Integration Disorder may continue to display the "odd" or "different" behaviors that many friends, relatives or professionals assured parents would diminish. Often these behaviors become even more pronounced. A pre-schooler who dislikes the playground, or will only go on the swings, may now be crying out that she is having problems integrating vestibular stimuli. Or, what about the child who desperately wants friends, but whose tactilely defensive behaviors turn other children away. Or, the pre-schooler whose sense of proprioception is so poor that he looks at a table with several empty chairs and says "there is no room for me." Most of us can still remember the child who ate like an animal, spoke in a booming voice, or was constantly tripping over air. Many grandparents tell tales of the little boy down the block who was four and a half years old, but screamed like a baby when his mother wiped his face.

While it is usually during the pre-school years that speech, fine or gross motor delays become more obvious, keep in mind that Sensory Integration Disorder is truly a hidden disorder. To the casual observer, a child with this disorder can appear either totally normal or just slightly different. What can be particularly deceiving is that many of these children go unnoticed by compensating for their deficiencies. This is especially common during the pre-school years, as most play--either at school or at home--is self-directed. Even most of the more "structured" environments for three and four-year-olds offer a choice of activities. Thus, the child with sensory integration difficulties may simply avoid certain activities and approach only those activities where her sensory systems are functioning efficiently enough to feel comfortable.

Because the symptoms of Sensory Integration Disorder are often subtle, some children with sensory integration problems do not exhibit extremes of behavior or seem delayed enough in any one area during the pre-school years to warrant an evaluation. However, if parents have concerns about their child, it is at this time that they may need to reject the perfunctory "wait and see" approach, and request an evaluation.

In contrast, other pre-schoolers with Sensory Integration Disorder have more obvious delays and exhibit extremes of behavior. As a result, it is at this time that many children receive their first evaluations. Delayed speech, fine motor or developmental delays are often the first concerns to be addressed by professionals. Often an evaluation in one area will lead to an evaluation in another area, until finally, the pieces of the puzzle can be put together and a diagnosis made.

School Age

If Sensory Integration Disorder goes undiagnosed beyond the pre-school years, chances are that the child, teacher and parents are feeling unhappy and frustrated with the child's progress. Many behavioral problems and learning disabilities have at their root an underlying sensory integration problem. These are often the children who cannot sit still because they are constantly making postural adjustments, or who cannot pay attention in class because the level of noise and activity in the room makes it difficult for them to prioritize and process sensory input. In order to cope other children may "shut down" and appear excessively bored or lethargic. Some children will sit out at recess because they are too overwhelmed to join in--the playground equipment provides aversive stimuli, while other children gravitate exclusively to a certain piece of equipment or area of the playground--craving its particular form of stimulation. Or, some children may have difficulty reading due to problems processing visual input. Other children may have difficulty with auditory processing. These children may have difficulty comprehending or following multiple-stepped directions.

Because the sensory systems are the foundation for learning--academically, emotionally and socially, any portion of a system that proves to be weak or inefficient will manifest in difficulties at school. Some of the most obvious manifestations of these difficulties are behavioral problems. These problems may range in severity from "stubborn," to uncooperative, to a down right refusal to participate. While these behaviors are often misinterpreted as willful disobedience, remember, a child with sensory integration difficulties is frantic to avoid certain sensations. In fact, he may become so frantic to avoid these sensations, that ne is willing to be "punished" time and time again for the same offenses.

Many school-aged children with Sensory Integration Disorder feel inadequate and beleaguered. Most children this age want so desperately to please adults and to fit in socially with their peers. But, when a child has sensory integration issues, he often must make a choice between pleasing an adult or experiencing aversive stimuli; between having a friend or keeping the weak structure of her world intact.

The bottom line is that acquiring all of the necessary academic skills to succeed in school is greatly impaired by Sensory Integration Disorder. A child who is receiving therapy, or some other form of appropriate intervention, has a fighting chance to overcome the many challenges of this disorder, a child who goes undiagnosed or without treatment does not.

The Undiagnosed Child - a Legacy of Failure

What about the child who goes undiagnosed? This is one possible case scenario. As an infant this child was considered unpredictable, demanding, or difficult. The toddler years were an unhappy period of tantrums, tears and "defiance."

As a pre-schooler, this child did not fit in socially. This is the child who cried because his classmates preferred to pack into other vehicles, rather than to ride in his van with him on a field trip. This is the child who desperately wanted friends, but whose behaviors turned away any potential friends. This is the pre-schooler who had a meltdown every time he, or anyone else, spilled a drink or food at snack time. This child could only be described as easily frustrated and moody. He was happy for only very short intervals. He was the four-year-old who feared the slide and seemed to trip over air. He was able to recognize all the letters of the alphabet, and distinguish colors, but could not effectively finger feed himself. By the time he left pre-school, his feelings of inadequacy were obvious.

What about this undiagnosed child when he entered kindergarten? He was the child who was very active and would not sit still or be quiet. He was the child who fell apart like a two-year-old whenever there was a change in routine. He was the child who refused to use the finger paints or play dough. He was the child who had no orientation to a pencil, or scissors, no matter how often he "practiced." He was the child who could not stack blocks to form a tall tower. By the end of kindergarten, he had a total lack of self-esteem.

In the later elementary grades this child was deemed a behavior problem. His social skills were so weak that he had difficulty making and keeping friends. He continued to fall apart over minor incidents. He read very well, although his writing was completely illegible. While he was quite verbally advanced, he had difficulty following simple instructions. By the end of elementary school, he had begun to realize how "different" he was from his peers. His peers had begun to echo this sentiment.

During his middle school years, he was characterized as "weird" by his peers. While he continued to read well beyond grade level, and could tell interesting and imaginative stories, he continued to write like a pre-schooler. Although he was fiercely competitive, he was always the last one to be chosen in gym class. By the end of middle school, he felt completely left out.

As a high school senior, he was considered by some to be very engaging yet "different." He was a member of the track team and photographer for the yearbook. His handwriting was illegible and thus he began to type instead of writing. By high school graduation, he had begun to take stock of his deficits and recognize his strengths. At this point, he also began to realize that his "life decisions," would be more complex.

The Symptoms

The following is a checklist of possible signs that a child may have Sensory Integration Disorder. It is by no means inclusive. The purpose of this list is to provide a brief overview of some of the behaviors most commonly associated with sensory integration problems. Keep in mind that some of the behaviors listed below, by themselves, do not necessarily point to a diagnosis of Sensory Integration Disorder. Not every learning disability has an underlying sensory disorder. On the other hand, just because a child has already been diagnosed with a learning disability does not mean that this same child does not also have sensory integration issues. While sensory integration problems manifest themselves somewhat differently in each child, the following symptoms may indicate that this disorder is present:

1. Overly sensitive to touch, movement, sights or sounds
2. Under-reactive to sensory stimulation
3. Activity level that is unusually high or unusually low
4. Coordination problems
5. Delays in speech or language skills
6. Delays in motor skills or academic achievement
7. Poor organization of behavior
8. A poor self-concept

What are the main characteristics of a child with a Sensory Integration Disorder? What red flags should parents be aware of that might indicate that their child, or a child they know, may have a sensory integration problem?

1. Overly sensitive to touch, movement, sights or sounds.

These symptoms can be seen in behaviors such as irritability or withdrawal when touched, strict avoidance of certain clothing or foods solely on the basis of texture, and a fearful reaction to ordinary activities such as bathing or brushing teeth.

2. Under-reactive to sensory stimulation.

A child who is under-reactive to sensory stimulation will usually seek out sensory experiences. For example, a child with an under-responsive tactile sense may constantly have his hands all over you. This child might also seem oblivious to pain. Some children even fluctuate between being under-responsive and being over-responsive.

3. Activity level that is unusually high or unusually low.

This behavior can be seen in the child who is constantly on the move and appears to be "all over the place" or, in the child who fatigues easily and is difficult to motivate. Again, a child can fluctuate between the two extremes.

4. Coordination problems.

These problems can be seen in either a child's gross or fine motor activities, or both. In addition, some children will have exceptionally poor balance and experience great difficulty learning to do something that involves motor planning.

5. Delays in speech or language skills.

Because speech and language problems are more obvious, they are often the first concerns about a child's development to be addressed. It is not uncommon for the parents of a child with Sensory Integration Disorder to have their child initially evaluated for a possible speech delay, only to learn that the child is having difficulty in other areas as well.

6. Delays in motor skills or academic achievement.

Since most schools shy away from any formal measure of academic achievement at the elementary level, these symptoms are usually seen when a child participates in projects where scissors, paint brushes or markers are used. If a pre-school has an indoor or outdoor play area, delays may also show up when the child uses the playground equipment. In an older child, there are usually problems with academic achievement despite the child testing within the range of normal intelligence.

7. Poor organization of behavior.

The child may be highly distractible, especially in a group setting, and might be described as "all over the place." In addition, the child may show a lack of planning and therefore appear extremely impulsive. A child may have trouble adjusting to new situations or react to failure with frustration, aggression or withdrawal.

8. Poor self-concept.

Because of the complex nature of Sensory Integration Disorder, a child does not only feel "out of sorts," the child can, and usually does, feel downright awful. As A. Jean Ayres wrote in her book <u>Sensory Integration and the Child</u>, there are three things that contribute to this negative self-image: "the way in which the nervous system is functioning, the feelings of frustration and inadequacy that arise when a child cannot do things well, and other people's negative reactions to what the child does."[1] Most children with sensory integration problems are well aware that some tasks are more difficult for them than they are for other children, they just don't understand why.

[1] A. Jean Ayres, <u>Sensory Integration and the Child,</u> p. 161

Some Common Sensitivities and Symptoms

The following lists provide a more detailed collection of possible symptoms and sensitivities of Sensory Integration Disorder. Because this disorder manifests itself differently in each child, these lists serve only as a sample. They are by no means inclusive, and do not necessarily mean a child has this disorder, only that a further evaluation by a licensed professional may be in order.

Motor Planning

·   difficulty climbing in and out of cars
·   difficulty going up and down stairs
·   falls out of chairs
·   walks into objects
·   difficulty using "pull toys"
·   problems using tricycles, bikes or Big Wheels
·   continues to have accidents after being fully potty trained
·   trouble engaging successfully in sports
·   approaches an activity each time as if it were the first time
·   strong preferences or aversions to playground equipment
·   difficulty doing puzzles----manipulating pieces or determining where pieces belong
·   difficulty guiding food to mouth
·   unable to use scissors as age appropriate

Clothing

·   strong clothing preferences
·   dislikes sleeves hitting wrists / only wears long or short sleeves
·   sensitive to collars hitting neck
·   does not want to wear a belt or anything that ties around the waist
·   is bothered by seams in clothing
·   prefers cotton
·   experiences difficulty manipulating buttons, zippers, snaps or ties
·   wants all tags in clothing removed
·   either wants feet and body totally covered or uncovered
·   insists on wearing a coat with the hood up in spite of hot weather
·   insists on wearing a T-shirt in spite of cold weather

Food

- sensitive to temperature
- sensitive to texture
- heightened awareness of flavor / lack of awareness of flavor
- difficulty manipulating eating utensils
- frequently spills both food and drinks
- chews with mouth open
- bites fingers and tongue while eating
- dribbles food and drink down chin
- drops food on the floor unintentionally
- dislikes carbonated beverages

Self-Care Skills

- dislikes brushing teeth
- dribbles toothpaste out of mouth, down chin, onto clothes
- avoids washing and combing hair
- avoids having fingernails and toenails clipped
- problems self-dressing
- trouble locating opening for sleeve in shirt
- puts shirt on backwards
- places two legs in one pant leg consistently
- difficulty with zippers, buttons or snaps
- difficulty pulling on socks and shoes
- problems learning how to tie / buckle shoes
- dislikes having nose and ears cleaned
- aversion to having feet touched
- under responsive or over responsive to the need to urinate or defecate

Muscle Tone

- poor posture
- poor strength and endurance
- rests head on hands often
- legs hang, rather than wrap, around someone's hips when carried
- distorted sense of heaviness when carrying things
- difficulty grasping and holding objects for any length of time

Temperatures

- sensitive to air and object temperature
- prefers luke-warm or cold foods or baths / prefers unusually hot foods or baths
- lack of awareness / heightened awareness of body temperature
- overdresses or under dresses for the weather

As a Child

- easily distracted
- difficulty prioritizing stimuli
- problems following directions
- dislikes sudden changes in plans and routine
- poor speech or articulation
- stubborn
- erratic sleep patterns
- sensitive to loud noise and commotion
- craves touching / avoids touching
- unusually high or unusually low energy level
- "falls apart" on a regular basis
- difficulty making choices when confronted with several options
- immature
- short attention-span in group setting /good attention span as an individual
- may appear clumsy or "spacey"
- impulsive
- may speak unusually loudly all the time
- distorted perception
- misses when placing an object on a table
- bumps into people and things

Early Diagnosis

The Importance of the Child's Placement Within the Family

While concerns about a child's development may come from a pediatrician, pre-school teacher or day care provider, they are usually first expressed by parents. As the ones who know their child best, parents are usually better able to judge when their child may be struggling.

If parents have concerns about their first child, early diagnosis of Sensory Integration Disorder can be hard to achieve. One reason for this is that with a first child, it can be even more difficult for parents to tell which behaviors are within the norm and which are not. Many parents shy away from comparing their child with other children that age. But, if there are concerns regarding the development or behavior of a first child, this can be the best place to form observations and gain perspective. Secondly, if parents meet any resistance in having their concerns addressed, a lack of prior parenting experience can make first-time parents more apt to lose their self-confidence and back down.

The early diagnosis of Sensory Integration Disorder is often somewhat easier when there are siblings. While every child in a family has his own personality, siblings do provide a day-to-day means of comparison. While every child develops at a unique pace, if there is a developmental delay or unexplainable behavior, it will usually be more obvious to parents who have other children.

The Role of Denial

One major cause for delay in the early diagnosis of Sensory Integration Disorder is denial. This denial may come in any one, or a combination, of three forms: self, family or professional.

While parents may be the first to sense that there is a problem with their child's development, they may also be the first to go into denial concerning this very problem. For the mother, sometimes this denial stems from a subconscious guilt over something that happened during pregnancy or that occurred in the delivery room. Many mothers of children with Sensory Integration Disorder will later feel that there was something they did that gave their child this disorder, or that there must have been something they could have done differently to prevent it. Fathers often experience their own form of denial. For fathers, this denial often generates from the feeling that having a child with this disorder is a difficult fact to accept.

A second type of denial is family denial. This form of denial usually occurs when one parent comes forward to their spouse, or extended family, with specific concerns about a child. These concerns are then either ignored or minimized by a family member.

A third type of denial, which can be by far the most difficult to overcome, is professional denial. While this issue will be addressed in depth later in this book, it is important to be aware that when parents confide in a professional, they may simply be reassured that it is best to take a "wait and see" approach.

Regardless of where the denial takes place, the outcome is usually the same...time is lost that could be best used to evaluate, diagnose, or treat a child. This valuable time could be spent in therapy helping a child succeed to the best of her ability. By continuing to deny that a child is experiencing problems, parents may, unknowingly, perpetuate a false sense of normalcy at the expense of the child.

It stands to reason that the more one is unfamiliar with something, the less likely one is to recognize its symptoms and therefore take action. A reason why many parents, teachers and pediatricians deny that a child may be experiencing a sensory integration problem is a lack of education concerning the symptoms and diagnosis of Sensory Integration Disorder.

Aside from this lack of education, what also makes the early diagnosis of Sensory Integration Disorder difficult is that this is truly a hidden disorder. With this disorder, a child may appear normal, or, as is very often the case, the symptoms are easily confused with those of other learning disabilities. Another factor which makes sensory integration problems hard to diagnose is that in addition to appearing normal, the child's behaviors may simply not be extreme enough to attract attention. In this case, a child may slip through the cracks until the problem manifests itself more blatantly later, usually in the form of an academic deficiency.

The Importance of Early Diagnosis

The early diagnosis of Sensory Integration Disorder is absolutely critical. Ages three through seven are the time when the brain is most receptive to sensations and is best able to organize them. The higher intellectual functions which occur after age seven depend on this earlier foundation of sensory integration. If, as is the case of Sensory Integration Disorder, this foundation does not develop naturally, it is imperative that a child receive therapy to foster its development. For it is only after this foundation is built that a child can successfully continue on a path toward intellectual, social, and personal development.

Achieving an Accurate Diagnosis

The pediatrician is usually the parents' first source for information regarding their child's medical or behavioral problems. However, when many parents go to their pediatrician with concerns over "odd" behaviors or possible developmental delays, they may only hear confident assurances that the child is just a late bloomer. If parents feel strongly that there is truly cause for concern, then they must either switch pediatricians or convince their current one to take them more seriously. Before deciding on a course of action, keep in mind that many pediatricians are willing conduits. Upon request, many physicians will make a referral to an occupational, physical or speech therapist for an evaluation, just as they will make a referral to a pediatric neurologist, allergist or psychologist. Parents seeking answers may need to ask for referrals to some, or all, of the above professionals.

A second option for parents seeking an evaluation for their child is to ask their pediatrician for a referral to a teaching hospital or diagnostic clinic. The value of these facilities should not be underestimated. Most teaching hospitals and diagnostic clinics follow an interdisciplinary approach. That is to say, they will look at the child as a whole after fitting the separate puzzle pieces together. From the information provided by parents, the pediatrician and teachers, a diagnostic clinic or teaching hospital will decide what types of evaluations (physical therapy, occupational therapy, speech / language, neurological, etc.) the child should undergo. Once these evaluations are completed and the results are tabulated, a team of professionals will review the results and form a consensus. This information will offer parents a much more complete picture of what is actually going on with their child. While the individual pieces of the puzzle may appear meaningless on their own, once locked together, they can provide invaluable insight into a child, his or her behavior, and how the child will best learn in the classroom.

To help achieve an accurate diagnosis of Sensory Integration Disorder it is absolutely essential that parents keep a notebook on their child. This is imperative! A large notebook that can be easily divided into two sections works the best. The first section should contain all of the parents' observations of the child. Included in this section should be the child's height, weight and outstanding physical characteristics along with a detailed description of the child's behaviors. This section should also describe the child the PARENTS know to any reader. Any questionable behaviors should be logged with the date, time and duration of the behavior, as well as a description of the behavior itself. For example: "5/5/95---9:45-10:05 AM After accidentally tipping over an empty cup, Jay wailed at the top of his lungs while flapping his hands and prancing in circles. No amount of reassuring or comforting would stop this behavior. The behavior waned only after I stood silently next to him for 10 minutes."

The second section of the notebook should contain a chronological diary of any contacts the parents have made or continue to make. For example, "On 5/7/95 we visited our pediatrician and expressed concern regarding our child's odd behavior. We pointed out that our child is clumsy, will only wear cotton clothes, eat soft foods and bathe in luke-warm water. The pediatrician responded by saying, "He'll grow out of it; it's just a phase." Be it over the phone, in a classroom or with a professional, each pertinent conversation needs to be paraphrased and logged in this notebook. Details of any meetings should also be entered.

As parents begin this notebook, it is important to keep in mind how highly instrumental this information could be in obtaining the necessary services for their child. In fact, it may be this notebook that yields the information needed to properly diagnose the child. This notebook will also serve as a concrete reminder when a professional asks the parents questions about the child's behaviors or symptoms. It will also be indispensable when the parents attempt to coordinate meetings and information between various professionals. Remember, that while parents may know their child better than anyone else, no parent can recall all of the dates, times, behaviors, and verbal exchanges that have occurred at meetings, over the phone or during office visits. This notebook is very easy to keep up once it has been started, and will quickly become an invaluable possession.

Along with a notebook, parents should also set up a separate file containing any correspondence to, or from, professionals, all medical records and a listing of pertinent telephone numbers. In the often time-consuming evaluation process, this file could save the parents hours of exhausting leg work.

The System

While it is common for parents to feel overwhelmed and alone when first facing concerns about their child's development, it may help them to know that many other parents have come before them, with an infinite number still to come. Help is available. Perhaps the most difficult part of addressing these concerns is knowing where to look for this help and, once found, how to go about enlisting it.

After a referral is made, the next step is to have a series of evaluations performed by licensed professionals. Although agencies and early childhood advocacy groups vary from state to state, and even from community to community, a little perseverance almost always yields a source from which parents can obtain a free or low-cost evaluation for their child.

Usually, contacting the child's school district will get the process of obtaining services started. Remember, even though a child may not be of school age, the school district is still responsible for having parents' concerns addressed, or to steer them in the appropriate direction. Unfortunately, many districts may know which evaluations to perform if parents come to them with concerns about a child's delayed or unintelligible speech, but may not be as familiar with the route to take when concerns mirror the symptoms of Sensory Integration Disorder. If this is the case, a little insistence should get the district to arrange the proper evaluations. These evaluations may be performed either "in house" or through the use of an outside facility. If insistence does not seem to motivate the district, a referral from the pediatrician's office may be helpful.

Frequently a child who is displaying the symptoms of Sensory Integration Disorder will also display other neurological problems as well. However, just because a child has already been diagnosed with, for example, Attention Deficit Disorder, Autism or Cerebral Palsy, does not mean that the child may not also have Sensory Integration Disorder, or underlying sensory integration issues.

When a child exhibits symptoms of Sensory Integration Disorder, this child must be evaluated by a licensed physical or occupational therapist. As parents, do not be afraid to ask if the therapist performing the evaluations has had any training in the field of sensory integration. Many times a child will have to undergo a battery of evaluations: speech, occupational therapy, physical therapy, psychological and developmental evaluations are all common. Do not let the number or length of these evaluations be frightening. Each evaluation is presented to the child as an opportunity to "play." More often than not, the child will not want to leave the evaluation because she is having so much fun!

Once evaluations have been completed, a recommendation will be made by each of the evaluators. At this juncture there are several options and possible courses of action open to parents. Let's explore several of the more common case scenarios:

First case scenario: Let's say that one or more of the evaluators from a particular discipline makes a recommendation that the child receive therapy a set number of times a week for a specific amount of time per session. If the parents concur with this recommendation, then the child is on the road to receiving services. One caveat here, just because a recommendation is in place does not necessarily mean that the child will actually begin to receive services. Be sure to obtain in writing that services will begin on a specific date, at a specific site (hospital, school, daycare center, etc.) with a specific therapist. When it comes to receiving the recommended services, do not accept that the process of locating a therapist will be a lengthy procedure, or that the school year is almost over and services "can wait" a few months, or any other excuse. It is up to parents to demand that any recommendation be carried out as expeditiously as possible. If parents are being ignored, then by all means they should retain an attorney (Legal Aid has been instrumental in helping families who cannot afford legal counsel with such issues) and pursue the matter legally.

Second case scenario: no recommendations for services are made by the evaluators, but the parents genuinely feel that their child needs services. At this point the parents may want to seek out a local child advocacy group to discuss what other options are available. Frequently, parents find that a second, impartial evaluation will yield the recommendation needed to either obtain services for the child or to allay their concerns.

Third case scenario: The evaluators indicate that there is a "delay," but do not feel it is substantial enough to warrant services. This is a tricky situation. If the parents are not satisfied with this recommendation, then asking for a second, independent evaluation is in order. However, if the evaluators present a strong case and the parents are in agreement with the recommendation (of no services) then most likely a re-evaluation should be scheduled after a reasonable amount of time, generally 6 to 12 months after the initial evaluation.

Fourth case scenario: recommendations for services are made by the evaluators, the parents concur, and the child begins therapy. Here the "three month rule" may need to be instituted. The "rule," states that if there is not some progress within three consecutive months of therapy, the program may need to be reassessed. At this point the parents need to voice their concerns and request that another meeting be scheduled. A change in program, a change of therapist, or a new approach may be in order.

Perseverance is the key to wading through an often inefficient system. Parents must not give up if they have a "gut" feeling that something is amiss in their child and that some form of intervention is needed.

How the System Can Fail

While many children with Sensory Integration Disorder successfully enter "the system" and begin receiving an appropriate program of therapy, there are instances where this is not the case.

A factor which can threaten the quality of therapy for a child with Sensory Integration Disorder is lack of funding. No money...no services has become the reality for many school districts. In the financially uncertain times of the 1990s, many Special Education Departments are both under staffed and over budget. In order to keep or get expenses down, some schools have been forced to cut back on staff and to cut down on the amount of actual services rendered. This can be done in several ways.

In many school districts, the number of therapists has not increased proportionately to the number of students needing Special Education Services. Not only is the workload for therapists greater, but some districts are expecting therapists with little, or no, training in the field of sensory integration to provide therapy for a child with this disorder. Many therapists are also being required to share their work area, resulting in overcrowding. In addition to space constraints, different types of therapy may occur simultaneously in this area, creating a chaotic environment. In this type of environment the benefits from therapy for any child, especially one with Sensory Integration Disorder, may be greatly diminished.

Another reality faced by therapists is the potential inability to provide an appropriate program of therapy depending on the financial situation of the school district. Due to a lack of funding, many children with Sensory Integration Disorder are not receiving adequate services; twelve month programs are not being recommended and/or implemented, the duration and number of weekly therapy sessions are being compromised, and appropriate equipment is not being purchased.

These situations are difficult for both therapists and parents alike. Unfortunately, it is the people affected most by lack of funds, (the child, the parents and the therapist) who may also have the least input when decisions are made. If parents feel that the services their child is receiving are unduly compromised in any way, they must actively advocate for their child. As the child's advocates, parents should keep themselves informed of all Special

34

Education legislation, attend all school meetings pertaining to their child, and continue to wage the battle to obtain appropriate services for their child as long as they are emotionally and physically able to do so.

The World of the SI Child: A Different Reality

One reason the world is such an interesting place is that everyone has their own preferences...for some people it may be rock music, Italian food or pull-over sweaters. While most people have their favorites, substitutes will do in a pinch...folk music, Chinese food or a cardigan sweater. One area that really sets children with Sensory Integration Disorder apart from the norm is that their preferences are not just a first choice, but symptomatic of their disorder.

Because the brain of a child with Sensory Integration Disorder does not process sensory information well, the child's nervous system is affected. As a result, sensitivities from inefficiencies in the tactile, vestibular or proprioceptive sensory systems often transform strong preferences into rigid demands. Clothing and food preferences are two areas where this effect is most prominent in a child with this disorder.

One example of this is the pre-schooler who will wear one particular outfit and only this one outfit. If this outfit is unavailable (even the most favorite of outfits requires an occasional trip to the laundry), most children can be rationally talked into wearing something else. However, for a child with a sensory integration problem, not being able to wear a particular outfit can take on monumental importance, and no amount of patience will enable this child to see reason. For this child, it may be that this favorite outfit doesn't have a tag in the back that feels like a knife. Perhaps the outfit isn't tight at the waist, have sleeves that hit the wrists or a collar that rubs his chin. Bear in mind that these are very real concerns to a child with Sensory Integration Disorder. For these children, what they wear can actually mean the difference between coping and not coping both at home and in the classroom.

The second area where the heightened sensitivities and strong preferences of a child with Sensory Integration Disorder are evident is food. While many parents try not to spoil or cater to a child when it comes to food, few parents would intentionally serve a child food she dislikes. As a result, parents usually try to prepare a meal that appeals to all of the children being served. This saves parents both time and effort, and also introduces children to a variety of foods.

But what about the child with Sensory Integration Disorder, who is highly sensitive to the temperature, texture or flavor of food? For some children with this disorder, warm food feels burning hot, a crunchy texture make them gag, or a flavor is so strong they cannot eat the food, whether it is breakfast at home, snack at school, or dinner at someone else's home.

Because of the many symptoms possible with this disorder, the world for a child with a sensory integration problem is a confusing, frightening, and often lonely place. Even seemingly simple choices and tasks like where to sit, what to draw, or how to feel about something can present a challenge socially, academically and emotionally.

Day to Day with The SI Child

Once most children reach a certain age, they begin to reason abstractly. For a child with Sensory Integration Disorder, this ability can lead to intense feelings of confusion and frustration. "Why me?" "Why is every experience so different for me?" The child with sensory integration difficulties may wonder aloud about their "different reality," most adults just do not hear the child's musings... Why do ALL the other kids enjoy going to the playground? The swings are too scary for me. The slide is too high. The see-saw makes me cry. Why does it feel like a doctor giving me a shot when Dad trims my fingernails? Why can my little sister draw a snowman and I cannot? When my teacher tells us to do something, why can everyone else remember what to do and I cannot?...if adults only knew what to listen for.

Because many children with Sensory Integration Disorder have trouble coping with their feelings, they often manifest these feelings with inappropriate behavior: aggression, hysterics and emotional withdrawal, to name just three. What is important to remember when dealing with a child who has Sensory Integration Disorder is to look beneath the behaviors at the underlying causes. While this won't eliminate the behaviors, it can help both parents and other children learn to deal more effectively with them.

Day to day existence must be lonely for children who experience most stimuli differently, then process it differently. Who can be the mirror for their reality? Who experiences life the same way they do? Not their mother. Not their father. Not their sibling. Not their teacher. Not their peers. For these reasons, children with Sensory Integration Disorder may have trouble maintaining existing relationships and developing new ones. Because they experience daily life so differently, children with this disorder often feel there is something "wrong" with them and are at risk for developing low self-esteem. Parents of a child with Sensory Integration Disorder must therefore, work unceasingly to help their child develop a good self-image. Remember, each day a child with Sensory Integration Disorder struggles to fit in, keep up, and be accepted by their peers. Because of this, every small step must be considered a triumph. Perhaps talking to another child at pre-school, and having that other child converse back, may be considered a huge step forward. Perhaps for the school-age child this could mean getting through an entire lunch period without any incidents or being teased. Keep in mind that socially, these children are probably understood by a very select group of people, mostly adults who have prior knowledge of the disorder. The parents and the occupational and physical therapist have some insight into this child, the teacher and his fellow classmates most likely do not.

Issues at Home

For a child with Sensory Integration Disorder, the only sanctuary from this confusing, frightening, and lonely world may be the home. Ironically, it is the nature of these unpredictable children that makes them thrive in a predictable or structured environment. Children with this disorder tend to be emotionally labile and also have an extremely low frustration level. In addition, their maturity may be well below their chronological age. These dichotomies, as well as others, present many challenges to successfully managing behavior of a child with Sensory Integration Disorder in the home.

Being a child with Sensory Integration Disorder is not easy. Being the family member of a child with this disorder is not any easier. While living with this disorder can be stressful for a family, developing an understanding and a willingness to accommodate the symptoms of the disorder when appropriate may help to greatly reduce the level of this stress.

The Big Three: Meals, Baths and Dressing

Mealtime is a hectic time for most families. Mealtime in a family that has a child with Sensory Integration Disorder is often anticipated with a sense of foreboding. Perhaps, by respecting some of the sensitivities of the child with this disorder, it can at least become manageable. If the family is being served a hot meal for example, this child's plate can be allowed to cool. If utensils pose a problem, the food can be cut up for the child prior to serving the meal. Assigned seating may reduce stress, certain "favorite" utensils may need to be used routinely. If the activity level of the child is so high that staying seated for the duration of the meal becomes a problem, then sending a child on a legitimate errand half way through the meal may help. If spilling beverages is a frequent occurrence, using sippy cups or a straw can help. Remember, it is not the actual spill that can make mealtime so difficult, spills occur at every family's dinner table. The risk is that a spill (his or anyone else's) may set off a child with Sensory Integration Disorder into a downward spiral of behavior (crying, withdrawal, flipping plates). This can result in the atmosphere of the meal being ruined for the entire family.

Likewise, if bath time is a source of aggravation for both the parents and child, respecting the child's sensitivities can be extremely helpful. At bath time, parents might consider allowing the child to determine the temperature of the water or the water level in the tub. Allowing the child to choose a specific towel for drying may be helpful to alleviate some of the tactile concerns. Sometimes allowing a child with Sensory Integration Disorder to shampoo and rinse his own hair helps reduce stress. If the hair does not get completely clean, but the child gains a greater level of comfort with bath time, it is well worth it. Other children with Sensory Integration Disorder are absolutely unable to cope with having their hair washed, and it is better for a parent to do it for them, quickly and amidst the child's panic.

Here are a few "tricks" devised by parents to reduce stress during bath time: One parent discovered that her child's anxiety level was greatly reduced whenever her child was able to use a mirror while performing any activity, including washing her hair, soaping and rinsing her body. This Mom purchased a plastic infant crib mirror and attached suction cups to the back--voila, a portable mirror for the bath, sink, room etc. Another parent realized that her son was able to tolerate being soaped up and rinsed much better if the parent handed him a "magic soap potion" to lather on himself. Additionally, distraction techniques are helpful for children with sensory issues: blowing bubbles, singing songs, and special tub toys.

42

A goal for every child (and parent) is to become proficient at self-dressing. For a child with Sensory Integration Disorder, inefficiencies in the tactile, vestibular, and proprioceptive systems may hinder her from reaching this goal. Since the symptoms of Sensory Integration Disorder often lead to frustration, behavior meltdowns during dressing can be an everyday occurrence (if not several times a day) for this child. To help a child overcome these obstacles to self-dressing, parents have several options available.

One option is for parents to dress the child themselves, perhaps against the wishes of the child. The risk in doing this is that a non-verbal message may be sent to the child that he is in some way inadequate. At the very least, this option does not aid in the development of either self-dressing or coping skills, and may lead to an even greater physical and emotional dependence on the parents.

A second option is to allow the child to attempt to dress herself without offering any assistance. This method lends itself to a high probability of frustration and emotional overload for both the child and parents. Remember, self-dressing requires an integrated tactile system (how the clothes feel while being put on), proprioceptive system (buttons, snaps and zippers), and vestibular system (to coordinate body movement).

A third option, and often the most beneficial, is to offer guidance, coupled with a moderate amount of assistance. Perhaps parents can guide the child's arm so a sleeve can be easily found, or place a finger over the child's finger to provide the strength necessary to snap her pants. Often verbal reassurances from the parents are enough to overcome each obstacle.

What is most important is to develop a technique that fosters both independence and eliminates the "rush, rush" scenario that can be so debilitating for a child with Sensory Integration Disorder. Remember, a child with this disorder is often one who has difficulty making quick decisions, is internally disorganized, may have diminished strength or coordination, poor motor planning and be emotionally unstable.

Because a child with this disorder may face many obstacles to self-dressing, it can be extremely difficult for parents to determine when the child

43

doesn't want to, for example, put on shoes, or is actually unable to put on her shoes. It is important for parents to realize that they will see "typical" behavior (resistance, defiance, refusal) even in an "atypical" child.

Discipline

Discipline for the child with Sensory Integration Disorder must be like space age plastic--strong, flexible, portable and gentle to the surrounding structure. Most likely only a combination of different types of discipline will be effective for these children. Since many of their unacceptable behaviors are either symptomatic of the disorder, or, born out of a deep frustration, more innovative methods of discipline may be needed.

When a "typical" child acts up, this child can be held accountable for his behavior and disciplined accordingly. When a child with Sensory Integration Disorder "falls apart", and the behavior becomes unacceptable, remember it is important to discipline the child, not punish her for behavior over which she has no control. For example, if a "typical" child refuses to hold a parent's hand while crossing the street, a parent would most likely discipline this child by not allowing him to cross until he complies. In contrast, if a child with Sensory Integration Disorder refuses to hold a parent's hand, the parent has to stop, introspect on the refusal, and formulate another game plan. Perhaps if the child is known to be tactilely defensive, then holding onto a piece of the parent's clothing could be a solution. Keep in mind that if parents engage in a power struggle with a "typical" child, they may win. If parents engage in a power struggle with a child who has Sensory Integration Disorder, everyone loses.

The following are several traditional and non-traditional methods of managing the behaviors of a child with Sensory Integration Disorder:

One of these methods is "time out". A reason for the success of "time out" for a child with Sensory Integration Disorder, is that it can be enacted just about anywhere. Granted the supermarket is a difficult place to have to enforce a "time out", but it can be done. Here, a "time out" can occur either in the grocery cart or by standing next to it. Even just a minute or two of "time out" can provide enough time for the child to calm down, prevent a sensory overload, and allow everyone to proceed with the activity. Again, the emphasis is on managing the child's behavior, not punishing a child for behavior over which she has no control.

One alternative to the more traditional "time out" is coaching a child with Sensory Integration Disorder in deep breathing techniques. It is important to choose a time of relative calm to explain to the child that these are some

45

exercises to help him through a difficult moment. Explain this technique long before the "moment" occurs and the child is asked to use it. Practice the deep breathing until the child feels comfortable with it and she is able to perform on command. For instance, if the child begins to spin "out of control" when a friend is over, at this time deep breathing techniques may be used---even amidst the chaos. The entire playdate may be salvaged by implementing this technique. These exercises are designed to disengage the child from a situation and allow him to regroup. When deep breathing is well practiced, both the parents and the child may be pleasantly surprised at how well this technique can work to diffuse the next potentially volatile situation.

A third method for managing the behavior of a child with Sensory Integration Disorder is to employ the "stop the situation before it gets out of hand" technique. If parents are on the look out, they can recognize that many-- not all--but many, potentially volatile situations before they escalate into a sensory overload and a behavioral meltdown. Observe the child. Many times a child will begin to act a certain way just before a downward spiral of behavior occurs. Many situations are, after really looking at the child's sensory history, a sure bet for an overload.

An added benefit of this technique is that eventually the child can hopefully, begin to self-regulate. By learning which situations and stimuli set their behavior on a downward spiral, children with Sensory Integration Disorder can then increase their ability to successfully manage in many different situations whether or not a parent is there. However, until a child with this disorder is able to "stop the situation" on her own, it is important for a parent to take charge for her and act quickly. Removing the child to a peaceful environment is often the most successful.

One parent, for example, realized that her daughter became "unglued" at the same time each afternoon. This parent began to watch for the telltale behaviors indicating that her daughter was about to "loose it", and then ushered her to a "special" room prepared with a choice of quiet activities and a snack. Many children with Sensory Integration Disorder do not need this regime every day, but when necessary, it can help manage the behavior of a child with this disorder.

Many times managing the behavior of a child with sensory integration problems means waiting out the storm. Often a child will become overwhelmed and may simply lose control over his emotions or behaviors.   When this happens, the child is beyond reasoning with, and may need to be alone until the storm has passed.

Implementing successful management techniques is vital not only for the child with Sensory Integration Disorder, but the entire family. For, if the symptoms and sensitivities of a child with this disorder are not managed, every family member will be affected by the resulting downward spirals of behaviors. It is important to note, however, that as the child with this disorder grows and evolves, so must the techniques used to manage the behaviors.

Issues at School

The issues facing a child with Sensory Integration Disorder at school are extremely complex. Depending on their individual sensitivities and symptoms, developmental delays, and social skills, these children bring with them into the classroom their unique perception of reality. Add to this the demands placed on a child both intellectually and behaviorally at school, and the seriousness of these issues becomes apparent.

What makes school especially challenging for a child with Sensory Integration Disorder is that this environment expects him to process a wide range of sensory input simultaneously. Yet, for a child with this disorder, inefficiencies in sensory processing greatly impair his ability to do this. In the classroom, a child may be expected to follow directions, sharpen a pencil, and pay attention to a message on the PA system, while other children are talking and getting up and down from their seats. For a child who has difficulty processing sensory input, prioritizing stimuli and motor planning, the result can be directions that are not followed, a pencil half sharpened and the announcement misunderstood.

To compound these issues, a child with sensory integration difficulties often enters school with an inconsistent level of skills. In some academic areas a child with Sensory Integration Disorder may perform well above the norm, while in other areas, this same child may perform far below the norm. For example, some children with this disorder are able to read at the age of three and a half, but are unable to turn the pages of the book. Conversely, other children with Sensory Integration Disorder may be able to turn the page, but have difficulty developing pre-reading skills.

While parental involvement is essential to any child's success in school, it is a broad-based approach to education with input from parents, teachers and therapists that is most beneficial to a child with Sensory Integration Disorder. For example, one child with Sensory Integration Disorder was so disorganized in his behavior that he was unable to select one activity to focus on during "free play" at pre-school. During this time this child would wander around the classroom just watching the other children. His teacher described him as "detached" and perhaps mentally slow. Yet, when asked, this child could describe each activity in great detail! By the parents and teacher working together, a more step-by-step method of instruction was instituted for him and subsequently he was able to process the information "hands on" and participate in "free play."

Another issue which greatly affects school life is the emotional lability of many children with sensory integration problems. They may feel fine one minute and extremely frustrated or overwhelmed the next. A simple task at school that may take a "typical" child a few attempts to master may take a child with Sensory Integration Disorder hundreds of repetitions to even become comfortable attempting. The problem is that a child with this disorder usually knows she should be able to perform a task, knows how to do it, but cannot integrate well enough to complete it. The child may, in addition, be hindered by an inadequate level of fine or gross motor skills. In addition, social interactions that most children would take in stride can be emotionally debilitating to a child with Sensory Integration Disorder. Again, this child knows she is reacting differently than the other children but she cannot control her response. When all of this occurs on a daily basis in class, the emotional impact on a child is devastating.

As school activities become more demanding, without the support and encouragement of parents, teachers and peers, a child with Sensory Integration Disorder becomes at risk for failure. For some children with this disorder, the pressures of academics, athletics and a social life become too much for them and they may stop trying.

The Expanding Role of the Teacher

With more inclusion of the severely disabled child in the classroom and a greater emphasis on managing the behavior of the mildly disabled child at the pre-referral level, the role of the classroom teacher is expanding. It is no longer a question of whether a teacher will have a child with Sensory Integration Disorder in class, but when.

There is so much a teacher can offer a child with Sensory Integration Disorder. While the more obvious things include a more effective way to hold a pencil or a desk at the front of the room, the most important may be the fostering of this child's sense of self-worth.

While most teachers are aware that maintaining a focus on a child's strengths is a key factor in success at school, what she may not realize is that this focusing on strengths is **the** key factor for a child with Sensory Integration Disorder in achieving scholastic success. For so many children with this disorder, the emphasis has always been on their areas of deficiency...that he cannot use scissors, that she cannot zip her coat, that he cannot sit still during story time, that she cannot tolerate loud noises.

While it is extremely important that a child's deficiencies be noted as valuable diagnostic clues and as a means of evaluating progress, once noted, the emphasis must immediately shift to the strengths of this child, if he is going to be successful at school. Keep in mind, these are children who are already emotionally labile and whose deficiencies may on the surface far outweigh their strengths.

Therefore, not only is it critical that a teacher convey a sense of these strengths to the child with Sensory Integration Disorder, but that these strengths are recognized and highlighted early on. A child with this disorder may burst into tears when the boy at the other end of her snack table spills his pretzels; but she may also be the first child to offer to help clean up the spill. Or, perhaps a child with Sensory Integration Disorder may be frustrated to the point of tears when trying to write, but can tell the same story with tremendous imagery and an advanced vocabulary. Teachers need to recognize empathy and creativity, rather than just focus on the obvious behavioral immaturity or fine motor difficulties. As a child who already faces many obstacles to learning and may be at risk for multiple learning disabilities, a child with Sensory Integration Disorder is also at risk for failure in the classroom.

Behavior Management at School: Recognizing Patterns

One certain way to diminish the risk of failure in the classroom for a child with Sensory Integration Disorder is for the teacher to develop an understanding of what is going on in this child's sensory systems.   Patterns may become clear...on the way back from gym class there is usually aggressive pushing in line...after art class there is usually greater frustration with learning the next lesson...after occupational, speech or physical therapy, there is often fatigue or irritability.   Not only will recognizing these patterns indirectly help manage behavior in the classroom, but it will help tremendously with the development of this child's self-esteem. While pushing in line is clearly unacceptable behavior, a child with Sensory Integration Disorder must be disciplined for the action, not for behavior over which he has no control. Just as a downward spiral of behavior can occur in the home, it can occur at school. And, with it, a downward spiral of self-esteem that can contribute to academic failure.

For example, a child who is tactilely defensive gets bumped in line and shoves forcefully back. Already this child is feeling out of sorts and experiencing a "fight or flight" response. If this same child is then reprimanded in front of the class, a downward spiral of behavior may follow. After being reprimanded, a child with Sensory Integration Disorder may be confused. Remember, because of his disorder, he is internally disorganized. He most likely does not even make the deeper connection between the cause and effect -- why he reacts this way (shoving after being lightly brushed) and the child standing next to him would not. This child may wonder why other children are capable of managing themselves in line and he is not.

To best manage the behavior of a child with Sensory Integration Disorder at school, a teacher must step back and introspect on this child's behavior. If a "typical" child commits the transgression of shoving in line, a verbal reprimand would most likely be in order. "Jay, please keep your hands to yourself, there is no shoving in line." With a "typical" child, this verbal reprimand would also most likely be effective in limiting future incidents in line. For the child with Sensory Integration Disorder, this approach will most likely be disastrous. Keep in mind, again, that this is a child who is emotionally labile and perhaps already experiencing a poor self-concept. A reprimand like this for a child with this disorder will most likely be perceived by the child as public humiliation and personal failure. This perception on the part of the child may manifest in a downward spiral; failure to participate for the remainder of the day, increase in the undesirable behavior, or a tearful meltdown. This chain of events is the reason why it is so important for a teacher to modify his approach when managing the behavior of a child with sensory integration problems. One possible solution for this scenario may be: asking the child to come to the front of the line, or to depersonalize the situation, "I see that there is some pushing in line, please stop now," or just a "look" may be enough to stop the behavior.

The Family

In the 1990s, almost anything goes when it comes to what constitutes a family. It is not uncommon today for a child to be living with one parent, a grandparent, or with children from a previous marriage. No matter what the make-up of the family, there is a host of relationships within it. For the purposes of this book, only three types of family relationships will be discussed: the husband / wife, parent / child, and child / sibling. To the casual observer, these relationships may seem fairly straight forward. It is upon closer scrutiny that the complexities of these relationships become more evident.

Whatever the make up of a family, it seems normal to those in it. Whether a family has boys, girls, artists, athletes, or a child with special needs, the composition of a family is all its members have ever known. There is no doubt that the dynamics of a family with all boys or all artists is different from a family with all girls or all athletes. But, what about the dynamics of a family when there is a child with Sensory Integration Disorder? If you have a family that includes a child with this disorder, or know one, you need only to observe the dynamics of a family where all of the children are "typical" to know how dramatic the difference can be.

A quick glance at the recent divorce statistics is evidence that today's marriages are under stress. Financial problems, combined with the hectic pace of society, pose a constant threat to the stability of any marriage. However, even these demands do not compare with the stress inadvertently placed on a marriage by raising a child with a disability.

Whether the child's disability is physical, mental or educational, it can become an intensely emotional issue in a couple's relationship. While the severity of the disability will vary from family to family, there is a common denominator, heartache is heartache. Raising a child with Sensory Integration Disorder may bring about some of life's greatest joys, but it may also bring with it some of life's deepest sorrows.

Being the parents of a child with sensory integration problems is like dying and being reborn all at the same time. It is the death of a dream. The dream that every parent has during every pregnancy, that the baby will be absolutely perfect. Many parents of children who have sensory integration problems thought that their dream had come true, that their child was perfect. It was not until later that the parents realized that this dream child is still wonderful, just not perfect. Sometimes parents are left feeling betrayed by this realization.

At first it is hard to separate the feelings. A parent may feel betrayed by the child, the spouse, even by the obstetrician, all at the same time. Many marriages are irrevocably altered by the advent of a child with Sensory Integration Disorder. Anger, frustration and denial are just a few of the emotions that can surface in any family member after a child has been diagnosed. Or, indeed, these feelings can be present long before the child is diagnosed, yet exhibiting symptoms.

Husband / Wife

When a child has Sensory Integration Disorder, challenges to the marriage become even more pronounced. Good communication, support and trust become essential. Other factors such as guilt, helplessness, and chronic fatigue can also enter in. The cumulative effect of these factors on a marriage is staggering. One parent may feel isolated while the other is busy attending to the special needs of the child with Sensory Integration Disorder. At the same time, the other parent may feel overwhelmed with the responsibilities of meeting the physical and emotional needs of this child. While the list of scenarios goes on and on, every family situation is unique. The bottom line is that raising a child with Sensory Integration Disorder makes the tough job of making a marriage work even tougher. Many couples are able to surmount the proverbial wall, pick through the rubble and journey forth into new territory. However, some relationships cannot withstand the stress of having a child with Sensory Integration Disorder. For many stated and tacit reasons, the relationship dissolves.

This web may weave even further, as many single parents (or guardians) who have a child with this disorder can find themselves having difficulty in other relationships. In the case of Sensory Integration Disorder, the parent can become the focus of blame for the child's inappropriate behavior. When this happens, even friendships can dissolve.

Since the parent's relationship with each other directly affects their child with Sensory Integration Disorder, let's explore several possible case scenarios.

In the best case scenario possible, the parents have "made it" through the darkest times and their commitment to each other and their child remains strong. Both parents take an active role in the child's life. Each parent is able to "work" with the child and handle the outbursts and meltdowns. Each parent is in tune with the rhythm and pace of the family, knows when a spouse has had enough, and is able to take up the slack. The parents form a united front when dealing with teachers, therapists, relatives and the child. In short, these parents are pulling together heart and soul to give to their child and to each other what they need not only to maintain, but to grow.

Now, let's look at the situation where the parents are committed to staying together, but one parent ends up being the physical and emotional custodian for the child. Perhaps one parent remains in denial regarding their child's Sensory Integration Disorder or the parent harbors guilt or anger. Whatever the reasons, the child in this situation will become the fulcrum upon which the family teeters and todders. Parents who are not working in synchronization will not be able to maximize the benefits of their labors. Even if one parent is busying himself with "all" the other activities required to run a family (especially if other children are involved), the other spouse might feel lonely, frustrated or overburdened. When this happens, the child may, in time, feel unloved or unaccepted by one or both parents.

The most alarming of the possible case scenarios is the situation where both parents deny that the disorder exists and never even seek help for their child. Even when there is intervention on the part of the school, without at least some parental support, this child is almost doomed to a life of abject misery. Schools, peers and relatives will most likely view the child as a behavioral problem, or, at the very least, uncooperative and unpleasant. Saddest of all is that the undiagnosed child will most likely internalize these labels, and simply never live up to his potential.

Lastly, what about the single parent who really wants to help a child? This is a lucky child. A parent who either willingly or unwillingly shoulders the burden of raising a child with Sensory Integration Disorder alone will have a long row to hoe. But both the parent and child can reap many benefits from such an effort. The single parent must in many ways work even harder to develop a support network that will buoy him or her up during times of stress and turmoil. Single parents may also develop an even stronger bond with this child as they face Sensory Integration Disorder together.

Parent / Child

While the relationship between every parent and child is unique, there are inherent differences between a parents' relationship with their "typical" child and with their "special needs" child. The basis for this difference is the "problematic bond" which often develops between a parent and a child with any disability. While both the parent / typical child and the parent / special needs child relationships can be positive or negative, the difference lies more in the intensity of the relationship.

Because the emotional and physical needs of a child with Sensory Integration Disorder are often more demanding than those of a "typical" child, parents are apt to devote additional time and energy to this child. While parents like to think that they divide themselves equally among all of their children, in reality it is often just not humanly possible. By expending more time and energy, many parents hope to gain a better understanding of the disorder, and therefore help their child. This serves a very important purpose as it enables parents to better meet their child's physical and emotional needs. The child, in turn, is apt to look to one parent for understanding and guidance. Thus, the creation of a "problematic" bond.

When a mother of several small children was once asked which child was her favorite she replied, "the one who needs me the most at that particular moment." While a child with Sensory Integration Disorder may or may not be a parent's favorite, it is this child who often needs the parents most at any given time. A child with Sensory Integration Disorder is not one a parent can just "drop off," or a child whose parents can be confident will be successful in every new situation. While all children need love and support, this need in a child with Sensory Integration Disorder can seem constant. While it is rewarding to be needed, some levels of need can also leave a parent both physically and emotionally drained. While every parent needs a break, this is especially true for the parent of a child with this disorder.

Like all relationships, the one between a parent and a child with a disability changes and develops over the years. One of the greatest challenges to this relationship is knowing when it is time to dissolve a "problematic" bond and to forge a new parent / child relationship and ultimately one between an adult child / parent.

Siblings

This book has already provided a glimpse into the life of a child with Sensory Integration Disorder, now let's look at the life of a sibling to such a child. No matter what the birth order, the sibling(s) of a child with any disability is never the center of attention for long. The daily requirements of this child demand that family life centers around the child with the disability. Fair does NOT mean equal. Siblings of a disabled child learn this credo at a very early age.

Children are born with a wonderful ability to accept people for who they are. While they may be initially curious about a disability, they are far more interested in whether or not the person is genuine, treats them well, or is fun to be around. This is also true in sibling relationships. Since siblings are familiar with the symptoms, if not the name, of their brother or sister's disability from an early age, they are able to see beyond the disability. They may not always like or agree with the disabled sibling, but recognize them for who they are or what they are doing, not the disability itself.

Maybe because of the innate inequities in their lives, many siblings of a child with a disability also learn understanding and empathy at an early age. Often siblings can be observed patiently and lovingly helping their disabled brother or sister. Siblings can also contribute to the support and unconditional love that every child needs when facing trying times. The pride that can be seen on the face of a sibling when a difficult task is mastered by a disabled brother or sister is truly priceless.

As a result of these inequities, the sibling of a child with Sensory Integration Disorder often leads a more enriched and complex life. At an early age, this sibling may face confusion, frustration and anger as he comes to grips with the reality that his sibling has special needs. "Why can't my brother be normal?" "Why can't I act like my sister and get away with it?" "Why am I normal?" " Why does my sister go to therapy?" These are just a few of the questions a sibling of a child with Sensory Integration Disorder ask. Even though siblings may be able to see beyond a disability, it does not mean they are immune to the challenges of a sibling relationship. In fact, these challenges are usually greater.

If the sibling is older than the child with Sensory Integration Disorder, more may be expected of her. She may be asked to accommodate certain behaviors or to help this child perform certain tasks. An older sibling may also independently, or with guidance, feel a greater sense of responsibility to protect the child.

Sensory Integration Disorder also makes for unique competition between siblings. A sibling may have to cope with a sister or brother who is chronologically older and cognitively more advanced, but a developmental equal. Because of the emotional lability and the general unpredictability of children with sensory issues, the sibling(s) never know what to expect. For example, two siblings are sitting quietly playing when one reaches to get something and slightly bumps the sibling. Because this sibling has sensory issues, a "fight or flight" response ensues. Thus, the unsuspecting sibling has been yelled at, hit and chased. The entire episode is a complete puzzlement to the "normal" child, leaving this child confused, afraid and guilty. Often a child with sensory integration issues will need virtual silence in order to concentrate, yet will scream deafeningly when experiencing a meltdown. Imagine a sibling who must remain totally silent while their sister struggles to dress a doll. Then, if that silence is broken, the sibling with sensory integration issues begins to scream "bloody murder" and physically lash out at her "normal" sibling. These are extremely difficult dynamics to incorporate into any sibling relationship. In addition, a sibling may resent his developmental milestones not being celebrated as enthusiastically as are the child's with Sensory Integration Disorder.

When families have a child with Sensory Integration Disorder, there are undoubtedly many sacrifices to be made by the siblings. Depending on the severity of the disorder, these may include certain activities, and the parents' time and energy to name just a few. There is no easy way to explain these sacrifices to the sibling(s). A simple explanation that may help both parents and siblings is that the situation is not fair, but that, as parents, this is the best you can do. As one parent explained to the six-year-old sibling, "I know that it's not fair that your brother gets the "lion's share" of attention, but you need to know that I would do the same for you."

One benefit to a sibling relationship, when one child has Sensory Integration Disorder, is exposure to many different types of children and forms of disabilities. Many of these siblings will spend time in waiting rooms with, for example, a child with Autism or Cerebral Palsy. For these siblings, rehabilitation centers are frequented more often than the grocery store. Accompanying their brother or sister to speech, occupational therapy or physical therapy is simply a part of their life.

Another benefit is that siblings often develop an increased ability to reach beyond themselves to the needs of another. Sometimes this comes from being asked to help their brother or sister with Sensory Integration Disorder, thus creating a greater awareness of the needs of others. Being the brother or sister of a child with this disorder can also have a profound influence on a sibling's life. Ask many occupational therapist, for example, what it was that influenced them to choose that career, and do not be surprised if they had a brother, sister or close relative with a disability.

Children who have a sibling with Sensory Integration Disorder often take with them into adulthood many attributes acquired as a result of having a brother or sister with this disorder. Tolerance, strength, and flexibility are just a few qualities that may serve siblings well throughout their lives.

Decisions

Decision-Making

Decision-making is part of parenting. Each day, parents are faced with a variety of decisions regarding their children. Some decisions are under consideration for a long time before they are actually made, while others are more immediate. Most parents agree that it is not always easy to make decisions for children. Regardless of their nature, most decisions have consequences. If a decision turns out to be a good one, the consequences are usually positive. If a decision turns out to be a poor one, there can be negative effects.

Some decisions, such as whether or not a child should nap, or have a coat on to go outside, seem minor. Others, pertaining to education or discipline, are usually considered most serious in nature. While making decisions for any child can be difficult, making decisions for a child with Sensory Integration Disorder can be overwhelming.

Why do so many parents of a child with Sensory Integration Disorder approach decisions with such trepidation? Perhaps it is a fear that their child may not rebound as quickly as a "typical" child. Or, maybe it is the result of an underlying desire to want to make "everything right" for a child who already faces many obstacles. There are a number of reasons why parents have difficulty making even small decisions for a child with sensory integration problems. When decisions are made on the spot, parents rely on prior experience to guide them. What can be disconcerting for parents of a child with Sensory Integration Disorder is that what has worked in the past might not work again.

Who to Tell

While each family situation is different, there are several big decisions that are faced by parents of a child with Sensory Integration Disorder.

One decision is who to tell and who not to tell about a child's disorder. Family background, current frame of mind, and advice from family, friends, physicians, and teachers will all enter into this decision.

Some parents feel very strongly that word not get out about their child's sensory integration problems. In contrast, other parents treat the disorder as simply part of their child's make-up. There are pros and cons to both mind sets. Not telling people about a child's sensory integration problems can eliminate awkward questions and might allow the family to "blend in" a little better. However, by not sharing that they have a child with Sensory Integration Disorder, parents also distance themselves from the emotional support and networking of information that can be invaluable. It should also be noted that there often comes a time, usually around Kindergarten, when it becomes obvious to outsiders that a child has some type of learning disability, whether or not parents have volunteered this information.

One question parents of a child with Sensory Integration Disorder might ask themselves is, "Will telling this person enhance her ability to work with my child?" The answer is probably "yes" if the person is a teacher, coach, care giver, or anyone who sees the child on a regular basis. The answer is probably "no" if this person is giving a one-time group lesson, the parent of a casual acquaintance, or someone whose contact with the child is limited.

If parents decide to be open about their child's sensory integration problems, they do risk setting their child up for intense scrutiny. For example, if a parent shares with a teacher that their child has been diagnosed with Sensory Integration Disorder, one of two things can happen: Either the teacher will work with the parents and therapist to form a team, or, the teacher may begin to regard the child as a "problem" and subconsciously develop a prejudice toward this child. To avoid this, it is helpful for parents to provide some written information on Sensory Integration when they share that their child has this disorder. The greater the understanding of the child's sensitivities and symptoms, the higher the degree of success this person will have.

Which School Is Best?

Another common decision faced by the parents of a child with Sensory Integration Disorder is determining what educational setting will be the most successful for this child.

Stage one of this critical decision usually occurs at the pre-school level. For a child with Sensory Integration Disorder, there are several options available: a regular pre-school with therapy on the side, an integrated classroom where therapy can be incorporated into the program, or, just therapy without pre-school. This decision is usually based on the severity of the disorder, what the parents feel is in the child's best interest, and if there is an individualized educational plan approved by the school district.

Stage two of this decision is whether or not to delay kindergarten (if this child is age eligible). For some parents, having their child in a full, or even half-day kindergarten where the child can receive therapy on site, is a necessity. For others, a decision to delay kindergarten by one year might provide the child with critical time to strengthen motor skills and develop maturity. Some parents have the option of a Developmental Kindergarten. If one is not available, parents might consider sending the child to an additional year of pre-school. Be aware that many school districts will strongly encourage parents to enroll a child with special needs in Kindergarten who is age eligible, and NOT to delay Kindergarten a year. Remember, the decision to enter or delay Kindergarten is a parental, not a school district decision. Since parents know their child best, it is important to go with your "gut" feeling. If parents decide to delay Kindergarten, their child, by law, is still eligible to receive services.

Once it has been established when a child with this disorder will enter kindergarten, then it must be decided whether the child will attend a public or a private school. While many private schools offer smaller class sizes, therapy may, or may not be available on-site. In contrast, a public school may have larger classes, but it must provide any approved services.

If a child's therapy is funded by the school district, the parents have a couple of options. They can send the child to a public school where the child will receive therapy at school during the school day, or they can send the child to a private school where the child will most likely receive services after school at another location. Family finances and district policy often play a large part in this educational decision.

Another common decision is in which activities to involve a child with Sensory Integration Disorder. There are many activities now available to children starting at the pre-school level: dance, karate, T-ball, and story time are just a few. Most parents want their child to participate in an activity to learn new things, strengthen existing skills, make friends, and have fun in the process. However, for the parents of a child with Sensory Integration Disorder, these positives are often tempered by the fear that their child may be exposed to undo stress, or even come away from the experience feeling he or she has failed in some way: as an individual, a son, or a daughter. It may be best to allow the child to choose the activity initially, but be prepared as parents to re-evaluate and "change course" if the activity is just not a success.

As parents face these decisions, interspersed among them are also decisions about family priorities and values, disciplinary procedures, and therapy, to name a few. While parents of a child with Sensory Integration Disorder may feel there is a barrage of decisions to make, it may help them to remember that they are not the first to face these decisions. Talking to other parents, especially to those with a child who has Sensory Integration Disorder, can relieve some of the stress.

Remember, when parents make decisions, they make them using their best judgment at that moment. People make mistakes. Remember that only hindsight is 20/20, and because it is uncharted territory, parents of a child with Sensory Integration Disorder may make even more than their fair share of mistakes. One parent uses the five-year criteria: "How will I feel about this decision five years from now? Will it matter that everyone in the restaurant gave disapproving glares when my seven-year-old son spilled his drink, then proceeded to have a meltdown? Or, that I decided to "wait out the storm" and simply ordered a new drink?"

Whether the decision turns out to be good or bad, what is important is that something is learned from it. It is only through learning that parents can reach a greater understanding of their child's disorder. The deeper the understanding, the greater the likelihood that future decisions will be positive ones.

66

Notes on Decision Making

1.   **Who will we tell about my child's Sensory Integration Disorder?**

     _____

     _____

     _____

2.   **What educational setting will be the most successful for my child?**

     _____

     _____

     _____

3.   **Will the school fund the cost of Sensory Integration therapy or will I need to find alternative funding?**

     _____

     _____

     _____

4.   **What Sensory Integration activities might my child be interested in?**

     _____

     _____

     _____

The Future

When a child is diagnosed with Sensory Integration Disorder and has begun therapy, parents may find their thoughts turning towards the future. "How long will my child need therapy?" "Will he always have difficulty with certain skills?" "Will this child be able to cope with increasing academic and social demands?" These are just a few questions that may keep a parent of a child with this disorder awake at night.

While it is natural to long for a crystal ball to gaze into for answers, there is no way to really know what the future has in store for a child with Sensory Integration Disorder. What makes this disorder hard to predict, is that it is constantly in metamorphoses. Some symptoms will completely disappear, some will seem less pronounced, others will manifest themselves differently, while new symptoms can appear at any time.

It is not knowing how the sensory integration difficulties will manifest that can seem overwhelming to the parents. Living with this uncertainty is like riding an emotional roller coaster. When the child has had a "good" day, parents often feel that their child's future is bright and that happiness and success are within reach. When the child has a "bad" day, the future can loom ominously. Despair over whether or not a child will ever have meaningful friendships or be able to adequately care for herself are common concerns.

One of the most effective ways parents can overcome feelings of anxiety is to recognize the disorder, gather resources, embrace the future and be as emotionally prepared as possible.

Resources for parents with a child who has Sensory Integration Disorder can come in a variety of forms: information in books, input from therapists, and discussions with other parents. For some parents, joining or starting a Sensory Integration support group is helpful. For others, support can be gathered from friends and family. Regardless of its origin, the point is that most parents of a child with Sensory Integration Disorder will benefit from some form of moral support.

While the benefits for parents of a support system are obvious, the benefits for the child are also plentiful, only more subtle. How parents feel about their child's disorder is often directly reflected in how the child feels. If parents have the resources necessary to cope with the demands of raising a child with sensory integration problems and are "O.K." with it, chances are quite good that the child will become "O.K." with it too. If parents feel that the future is bright for their child, it is likely that this is how the child will see the future also. Similarly, if the child knows her parents love her for who she is, not what she can or cannot do, this child's frustration level may lower, while her spirit soars.

No parent knows what is in store for their child. Parents of a child with Sensory Integration Disorder may be faced with this reality sooner. Because the future is unknown, a parent can only attempt to learn from the past, live in the present and hope for the future.

Dylan and Ellie's Stories

Here are the stories of Dylan and Ellie, two children who suffer from Sensory Integration Disorder. By sharing their journeys of pain, courage, perseverance and hope, it is possible to catch a glimpse into the life of a child for whom the world is a confusing, overwhelming, and often frightening place. It is also the struggle of two families who have been forced to create order from chaos and gain strength from weakness.

"Look Mommy, we're Super Heroes!" shouts my five-year-old from his swing. "I'm Batman and Ellie is Batwoman." My eyes fill with tears. "you ARE both super..." a lump in my throat prevents me from finishing the sentence with what is in my heart. You see, Dylan and Ellie are swinging from suspended apparatus in the Rehabilitation Department of a local hospital. The woman supervising their "play" is an occupational therapist who specializes in pediatric sensory integration.

Dylan's Story

After a trying pregnancy and a difficult delivery, Dylan was born to two elated, yet weary, parents. Right from the beginning, however, Dylan found touch to be aversive. He wanted Mom or Dad to be within sight, but did not wish to be cuddled. Dylan was constantly wakeful, taking only 20 minute "power" naps throughout the day and night. It was not until sometime later that I realized only 100% cotton clothing and NO blanket would result in his sleeping for longer than five minutes. Strangely, Dylan never became agitated when he was physically cold; he enjoyed it. For example, baths were luke-warm at best, otherwise, he would scream as though he were boiling in oil. Similarly, if his bottle or food were even warm, they would be rejected.

Throughout Dylan's infancy, I thought of myself as a first-time parent struggling with a "difficult" baby, or so that was what I was told time and time again by the people I was looking to for advice. Yet, even with these reassurances, I knew in my heart that the truth was not that simple.

It was upon reaching the toddler years that Dylan's odd behaviors became even more pronounced. No longer was he just "quirky." A strong feeling that something was really wrong began to gnaw at me daily as I witnessed Dylan's sensory problems amplify. While Dylan continued to demand cold food, cold baths and cold sleeping conditions, now anything with even a remotely crunchy texture would also be rejected. In addition, washing Dylan's hair was akin to a world class wrestling event. Because it was such an ordeal, my husband Dale flatly refused to bathe Dylan, and even avoided feeding his son. I was appalled to realize that I no longer served hot meals! Dylan's Sensory Integration Disorder had come to rule our lives, and we had never even heard of the term.

Unlike many children with Sensory Integration Disorder, Dylan reached most of his developmental milestones early. He crawled, sat with a straight back and cruised all on the day he turned seven months. By nine months Dylan was chasing the dog around the house at break neck-speed. When he was 17 months old, his sister Laura was born. While I was in the hospital, Grandma watching Dylan remarked, "He is so bright---he knows all his colors and shapes, and can recite the alphabet. He even tells me what he or the dog wants to eat for lunch. But he does act strangely for a 17-month-old." I had a new baby, a "difficult" toddler and an honest Mother.....I only could hope things would get better.

When the new baby got into a routine, I began to compare her behaviors to Dylan's at the same age, and grew increasingly alarmed. By the time Dylan was two and a half, I began actively seeking help. I was not sure exactly what was wrong, but I knew that some form of intervention was needed. Thankfully, I had the support of my mother and a couple of close friends. The first two or three "professional" sources I sought out were less than helpful. The tacit inference was that I wanted a perfect child and was therefore looking for something to be wrong. My break finally came when a non-judgmental neighbor suggested that if I had concerns regarding a pre-school child, I should contact the local Early Childhood Direction Center. I did just that the next day and was relieved to hear an informed and sympathetic ear. I was instructed to phone a local agency, and speak with someone about having Dylan evaluated by a developmental specialist and an occupational therapist. Appointments for the evaluations were set up, and much to my surprise, they were performed at no cost to me.

At age three Dylan began receiving occupational and physical therapy several times a week as a direct result of the evaluations he had undergone. As a pre-schooler, his sensory integration problems had become more defined and easier to pinpoint. Of course, it was also at this time that Dylan became one of the luckiest children in the world of therapy. His occupational therapist truly thinks he is special. Eileen loves him, and in turn Dylan absolutely adores her.

It was Eileen who assured me that I was not crazy when I described Dylan as being wired differently. In fact, I was shocked when Eileen would ask very pointed questions about Dylan's behaviors and then respond with a "that's what I thought you would say." She knew that even though Dylan hated to be touched, loathed swings, and practically went unconscious when asked to ride a see-saw, that he would seek out certain sensations in an almost obsessive way. This is a child who does not drink carbonated beverages, eat crunchy cookies , or consume a hot meal. Yet, the longer and faster the slide, the better. He loves the feel of the porcelain tub and actually asks to sleep there. But, this same child reacts to the rubber, textured bath mat in this tub as if it were a bed of thorns.

Dylan has waded out into the Atlantic Ocean with open blisters on his feet and not "noticed" whether his feet hurt or not. However, after his father placed bandages over these blisters, Dylan screamed hysterically for 10 minutes, when a stranger from a neighboring cottage came over to ask if we needed help. At this point we removed the bandages and Dylan stopped screaming. Just as he has a "different" awareness of pain, Dylan acts as though his legs are detached.

During baths, he will frequently ask, "Mommy, have my legs been washed yet?" to which I reply, "Honey, I just soaped them up and rinsed your legs---all done!" One of my favorite Sensory Integration stories about Dylan occurred when he was five years old. Dylan, Laura and I were at the local YMCA signing up for a class when things started getting out of hand and I asked them to please put their coats on NOW (before we were asked to leave)! A couple of minutes later I looked up from my paper work to see and hear a small crowd gathered around a child having a very loud tantrum. At that moment I realized that it was my son! I calmly walked over amidst the glares and asked Dylan what was wrong. He replied through the sobs, "Mommy, you told me to put on my coat, but I can't find it anywhere." It was at this point that I said to Dylan, "Look on your back, you're already wearing your coat." Dylan looked at his arms, saw his coat and replied, "Oh, I'm glad it's not lost!" and promptly stopped crying.

Dylan has worked very hard to overcome his sensory integration problems and has come a long way as a result of this hard work. Our family has also struggled. I think that we all realize now that our life will never be completely "normal," and that's okay. As a family we have made many sacrifices, but we have also made many gains. As a result of living with this disorder, Dylan and his sister Laura have developed great empathy for all people. They bring this compassion into every aspect of their lives. My husband and I have navigated through storm after storm and have not lost sight of the truth--that we have two wonderful kids and not everyone needs a hot meal.

"Old Man Joe"
By: Dylan Emmons
Age four

Old man Joe,
Old man Joe,
Sitting in the kitchen baking bread.
It makes his head feel better,
Feel better,
When he's doing the things he should do,
Ought to do.
But, sometimes, when I look into his eyes,
It feels like it's raining in my heart.

When Polly asked Dylan about the last line in this poem (she thought it was exceptionally "dark"), he responded that "rain can sound like so many different feelings--happy, sad, mad, afraid or sorry."

"Christmas Tree, Don't Go"
By: Dylan Emmons
Age five

Christmas tree, you have been
With us so long,
I don't want you to go.
I hope you have a good time
In the woods,
With the animals, buried beneath the snow.

"An Eagle's Claw"
By: Dylan Emmons
Age five

I wish I had an eagle's claws,
I could rip and tear.
My hands would be my friends.
To reach the joyous mountain peaks,
To fly there on my own.
I would have my claws with me there,
Even when I'm far from home.
But my hands don't work like that,
I guess that's okay,
I like to pet animals.
My hands can be soft and gentle.

Ellie's Story

Ellie has a nice home, she has fun toys to play with and good food to eat, she has a family who loves her... of these things I was certain. Yet, night after night I lay awake in the darkness haunted by the same questions. Why is Ellie so unhappy? What am I doing wrong? Where do I turn to for help? For the first time as a mother I felt totally unsure of myself, completely alone and desperately afraid.

Following an uneventful pregnancy and delivery I was thrilled with the arrival of my second daughter Ellie. It was a hot August and I envisioned picnics in the park and walks with the double stroller. Yet, I sensed almost immediately that there was something different about Ellie.

At Ellie's two-month check-up her pediatrician asked me how everything was going. I didn't realize how much I was struggling until I found myself sobbing, "She cries all the time and never sleeps. She gets so frantic in the carseat that she scratches her face until it bleeds. She screams in the front carrier and in the stroller. She doesn't nurse well and takes an hour to drink a bottle." Without realizing it, I had already begun searching for answers. With the best intentions, my pediatrician proceeded to remind me that some babies are fussier than others and to simply be patient. I knew I wouldn't find an answer that day and left his office with a sinking feeling I couldn't even verbalize to myself.

I began reading every parenting book I could get my hands on and cornered unsuspecting mothers at the playground. Willing to try anything, I sought advice from family and friends. But, as I confided in a friend when Ellie was a few months old, "No matter what I do, I can't comfort her. I worry that I will never have quality time with her older sister Lindy again. I can't get a break because I can't leave her with a sitter. My husband doesn't understand how I feel and thinks it's just an extended post-partum depression." It was as if someone had turned my world upside-down. Suddenly I found myself living in a house of needy people and I had nothing left to give.

So I focused on Ellie's next developmental step to provide that elusive turning point in our lives...maybe when she can crawl, maybe when she can feed herself...maybe when she can walk...Yet, instead of a clear turn in the road there were only rolling hills and deep valleys.

76

I knew from my first daughter that toddlers are unpredictable, but nothing had prepared me for Ellie's intense mood swings...happy one minute, huddled in the corner and hysterical the next. I lived on the edge, never knowing when something would set her off. Usually I did not even know what that something was.

As a family we began to tread lightly around Ellie knowing instinctively how weak the structure supporting her world was. Everything was a battle: washing and combing her hair, brushing her teeth, getting dressed, eating a meal, sharing a toy. Unlike her sister, who had shown typical defiance, Ellie's refusals to cooperate were desperate attempts at avoidance and completely devoid of reason. Not knowing what else to do, I punished Ellie. She cried and I cried. These were not tears of anger or hurt, but tears of sorrow. Ellie could not tell me what was wrong and I could not help her. A chasm was developing over which neither of us could reach. Having tried everything else, I stopped trying to "fix" Ellie's life or to mold her into the child I wanted her to be. In place of power struggles and tension, I gave her my love unconditionally. I knew how desperately she needed this; little did I know how much she deserved it.

At this time my third daughter Julia was born and in the increasingly loud, hectic nature of our household, Ellie sunk into a state of despair. While everyone played games at her older sister's birthday party, Ellie would sob on my shoulder. When friends came over to play, Ellie wandered around confused as if she did not know where to focus her attention. If the baby cried, Ellie covered her ears and hid. The lukewarm bath water felt burning hot; she couldn't tolerate the tags in her clothing, fell out of chairs, ran into furniture, spilled juice getting the cup to her mouth and was terrified when the car turned the corner. I continued calling friends and family and searching parenting books for advice. Deep down I knew that not only would I have trouble finding answers, but that when I did, they would be far from simple. I also knew that Ellie was like a little bird who wanted to fly, but did not even have wings.

The birth of my son Carter coupled with Ellie beginning pre-school finally gave me the means of comparison to validate years of concern. While I was continually reassured that Ellie was the easiest child in the class, I had only to sit and observe in the classroom to see that Ellie was indeed very different from the other children. Not only were there subtle developmental delays, but there was an immaturity, an inability to prioritize stimuli, and a difficulty processing language. It was at this point that I stopped asking questions and began demanding answers.

By contacting the director of Special Education in my school district, I was able to schedule a series of evaluations for Ellie. While fine motor and speech delays were obvious leads during these evaluations, the real answer I had been looking for came with a call from New Hampshire. A friend had heard about the trouble I was having with Ellie and wondered if she could ask me a few questions. After an hour on the phone, I stood in disbelief when this sensory integration specialist said "Liz, I think she's one of my kids." Here was a woman who could accurately describe Ellie's behavior without ever having even met her.

With this friend's guidance, I was able to locate an occupational therapist in my area, who is also trained in Sensory Integration. The success of Ellie's therapy has changed our lives.

How often I have wished I could go back in time and relive those early years with Ellie. If only I had known that her behavior was not the result of stubbornness, but a sensory integration problem over which she had no control. Those early years were a tough time not only for Ellie and me, but for our family. For her siblings, it was a time of uncertainty, There were days spent with a mother driven to distraction by phone calls to evaluators, therapists and special education personnel. While three days a week Ellie's two sisters and brother continue to make the trek to therapy, as a family we have come to accept this just as we have the trek to soccer games or dance class.

We have also come to accept Ellie, as we have all children, for what makes them special, not how well they fit into our mold. As a couple, Richard and I were forced to accept the death of a dream. A dream that we would have four perfect children who would simply glide through life. But, both of us have also been liberated from the confines of this very dream. For no child is perfect and no child escapes life's struggles. As a family we have been dragged unwillingly into the world of special education. However, it has also expanded our horizons in a way we never knew was even possible.

According to Ellie...

"When my fingernails are trimmed, each time a nail is cut it feels like the doctor is giving me a shot."

"I don't like to wear the dance leotard.   It burns my skin."

While Liz was outside painting one day, Ellie came running up to her saying, "I'm going inside to get my backpack... Then, I'm going to get my doll, a snack, and a blanket...Because, I'm going hiking in the back yard..." Liz heard the front door slam as Ellie ran inside. Immediately, she heard it slam again as Ellie ran back out. "Mommy, why was I going inside and what was I going to do?"

Riding in the car one day, Ellie's sister Julia called to her. "Ellie..., Ellie..., Ellie," Julia said. "What are you saying?," Ellie kept repeating. Finally, in total, frustration, Ellie turned to Liz and said, "Mommy, you have just got to get me some new ears. I can't understand a word she is saying."

"Guess what? When I'm outside and am thirsty, I don't have to come inside anymore for a drink because I can drink my tongue. See?" Ellie then swallowed efficiently -- probably for the first time in her five years.

"Daddy, I'm afraid of nightime." "Why Ellie?" "Because in the dark I don't know who I am."

What about Ellie and Dylan now? They both continue to receive therapy several times a week. Some of their early symptoms have disappeared, some remain and new ones have developed. Does therapy continue to make a difference in their lives? It certainly does. Dylan and Ellie are no longer just children struggling to be normal—they are Super Heroes, who enjoy sharing a swing.

Conclusion

We are all what we integrate. Processing information through the senses is not something that just children do. It is also not an all or nothing thing. Nobody's ability to process sensory input is perfect, and everyone has at least some difficulty. Our different abilities to integrate information through our senses is part of what makes us human; no two of us are exactly alike.

Some people are able to process certain forms of sensory input better than others and, as a whole, to integrate this information better or worse than the next person. Therefore, varying degrees of processing can be seen not just at the playground, but also at the amusement park. Not just in the classroom, but in the boardroom. Not just on the T-ball field, but at the ball park.

While some children suffer from Sensory Integration Disorder, every person exhibits subtle behaviors that indicate mild sensory integration issues. For example, some adults will wear only 100% cotton clothing, and it is considered a fashion statement. Others have a tremendous fear of heights, and it is called a phobia. People who have trouble writing may opt to use a computer, and those who have difficulty reading will be more likely to turn on the television.

Each of us processes information through the senses every minute of every day. When we are doing it well, we usually feel good about ourselves. When we are having trouble processing, we often do not feel good about ourselves. If we have trouble integrating, it will show up in our jobs, our relationships and in every area of our lives. Being aware that how we process information is what gives each of us our unique perception of reality. It will not only help us to cope with a child who has Sensory Integration Disorder but will also give us a greater understanding of ourselves.

Treatment Options

The following options are currently being linked by some to the successful treatment of Sensory Integration Dysfunction. Those who know the child best must decide which options are more appropriate to explore further. Remember, when a child receives a diagnosis (or therapy, or a "gut" instinct tells the parent that something is amiss), the parent must become the ultimate consumer. Read, ask questions, and become the most informed consumer possible.

Allergies

There is an abundance of allergy related treatments available for; environmental, food, and chemical sensitivities. Currently there are several approaches being used to diagnose and alleviate the symptoms of these allergies. Some of these include injections, inhalers, nebulizers and dietary changes.

Auditory Integration Training

Developed by a French physician Dr. Berard, this procedure makes use of different sound frequencies to exercise the ear, in order to desensitize and improve hearing.

Behavior Modification

Although there are many different types of Behavior Modification paradigms, The Lovaas Method is bandied about frequently, particularly in the field of Autism. This method attempts to eliminate undesirable behaviors by the use of shaping techniques.

Homeopathy

Increasing numbers of people are turning toward this treatment option. It advocates the use of natural ingredients and organic materials in treating illness and maintaining good health.

Osteopathy

This option is centered around the integration of the physical manipulation of the body with homeopathic components such as natural remedies in order to achieve and maintain good health.

Sensory Integration

Sensory Integration Therapy, in its various forms, allows a child to substantially direct the level and intensity of his perceived sensory stimulation. The intended goal is to build more efficient and integrated sensory systems.

Brushing: This protocol recommends the use of a specific type of surgical scrub brush. This brush is used on certain areas of the body, followed by joint compressions, to calm and integrate the nervous system.

Suspension Equipment: A variety of specially-designed swings and other apparatus are used to produce specific neurological responses in order to promote the integration of the sensory systems.

Visual Training

Visual Training is usually administered via a Behavior Optometrist. This option fosters the development of visual abilities in children as they relate to school performance. This method utilizes specially designed eye exercises and eye glasses to achieve its goals.

Vitamin Therapy

Vitamin Therapy is usage of specific vitamins and minerals, in specific dosages, in order to promote and maintain good health.

Glossary

The following glossary was devised by Liz and Polly. This is our attempt to demystify some of the technical terminology associated with Sensory Integration.

Developmental Delay: Occurs when a child is not doing what he or she normally should be able to do at his or her age or stage or development. For example, delayed walking.

Gravitational Insecurity: An unusual fear of movement which involves change in position of the head. For example, when a chair is slightly tipped (poor vestibular processing).

Kinesthesia: The conscious awareness of body parts in relation to movement. All the senses combine to give the brain information from inside and outside the body. For example, when you see a banana peel on the floor and bend over to pick it up.

Learning Disability: Characterized as difficulty learning school work (reading, writing, math), that is not caused by impaired sight, hearing or mental retardation, or inadequate parenting. For example, the reading difficulties associated with dyslexia.

Meltdown: Occurs when a child overloads from sensory stimuli, most often accompanied by sobbing, thrashing and screaming. For example, a child becomes overloaded at the playground and becomes completely uncontrollable and irrational, resulting in a child who has "checked out," and a parent who is leaving skid marks in the parking lot.

Occupational Therapy: The art and science of prompting and maintaining health through meaningful activity. For children this involves daily living skills such as: playing, dressing and feeding.

Physical Therapy: Learning an awareness of and training of large muscles involving strengthening, balance and movement. For example, learning how to walk after a leg injury, or stretching the leg muscles of a child with Cerebral Palsy.

Proprioception: Unconscious information from the muscles and joints about position, weight or pressure, stretch, movement and changes of position in space. For example, holding a pencil correctly in order to write.

Sensory Integration: Pertains to using our senses (hearing, sight, smell, taste, touch, proprioception, and vestibular) to allow the brain to organize this information and respond appropriately. For example, the age appropriate use of playground equipment.

Speech Language Pathology: The integration of articulation, language processing, and oral motor abilities. For example, eliminating disfluency, or learning to chew and swallow effectively.

Tactile: Pertaining to the sense of touch. For example, the feeling of a towel on your skin.

Vestibular: Encompasses the unconscious information from the inner ear about equilibrium, gravity, movement and changes of position in space. For example, swinging.

Resources

The following is a list of some of the more widely known resources we have used to gather information and publication lists on Sensory Integration Dysfunction:

American Occupational Therapy Association Inc.
P.O. Box 31220
Bethesda, MD 20824-1220

Developmental Delay Registry
6701 Fairfax Road
Chevy Chase, MD 20815

Sensory Integration International
P.O. Box 9013
Torrance, CA 90508

Bibliography

Ayres, A.J. (1979). *Sensory Integration and the Child.* Los Angeles: Western Psychological Services.

About the Authors

Elizabeth M. Anderson, MA, was raised in Connecticut and now lives in Binghamton, NY with her husband, Richard. They have four children: Lindy, Ellie, Julia and Carter.

Pauline A. Emmons, B.S., B.A., was raised in New York State and now lives in Binghamton, NY with her husband, Dale, and their two children: Dylan and Laura.